# THE
# SWEETS
## ═BOOK═
### Home-made sweets,
### chocolates and candies

# THE
# SWEETS
## ═══BOOK═══
### Home-made sweets, chocolates and candies

## SHONA CRAWFORD POOLE

Photography by Jasper Partington

Collins
8 Grafton Street, London W1X 3LA
1986

*For Janet and Crawford*

First published in Great Britain 1986
by William Collins Sons & Co Ltd
London · Glasgow · Sydney
Auckland · Toronto · Johannesburg

*Line drawings by Kate Osborne (decorative) and Aziz Khan (practical)*

*British Library Cataloguing in Publication Data*
Poole, Shona Crawford
    Sweets book.
    1. Confectionery——Juvenile literature
    I. Title
    641.8'53      TX791

ISBN 0-00-218151-7

Photoset by Rowland Phototypesetting Ltd,
Bury St Edmunds, Suffolk

Colour originated by Adroit Photo Litho Ltd, Birmingham

Printed and bound by
Wm Collins Sons and Co Ltd, Glasgow

# Contents

## Acknowledgements

Detail of *Summer in Cumberland* by James Durden, reproduced by courtesy of the Board of Trustees of the Victoria and Albert Museum.

Clarice Cliff plates from the collection of Dr and Mrs Nathaniel Cary.

Detail of *Snowballing* by John Morgan, reproduced by courtesy of the Board of Trustees of the Bethnal Green Museum of Childhood.

*Brightest London,* poster design by Horace Taylor, reproduced by courtesy of London Regional Transport.

Pears Soap print from the collection of Glynn Christian.

Detail of *For the riverside: Teddington Lock* by H. M. Wilson, reproduced by courtesy of London Regional Transport.

# Introduction

On the scale of childhood pleasures that rated Christmas, birthdays, Halloween, and a grandmother coming to stay simply dizzying, making sweets was very nearly as exciting. There is a mixture of anticipation and impatience that amounts to a thrill, and toffee making demands all the patience a seven-year-old can muster. The sugar seemed to take an age to melt, but at least we were allowed to hasten it along with a stir. Then, once it came to the boil, stirring was forbidden. Impatience grew until, after what seemed another age although it can only have been a few minutes, we were allowed to test a few drops of the boiling syrup in a mug of cold water to see if it was chewy yet, or brittle. It depended on what we were making. For fudge or tablet a syrup which stiffened into a chewy ball on contact with the water was just right. For treacle toffee it could be harder, or even brittle.

Thermometers played no part in the sweets my brother and I helped (or hindered) our mother and grandmothers to make. Equipment and ingredients were basic: the tools were a large, heavy pan, a wooden spoon and a tin to pour the toffee into to set. Molasses, syrup, brown sugar, milk, butter, nuts, raisins, cocoa and vanilla are the only ingredients I remember using.

When I began collecting the recipes for this book I had neither made nor eaten those childhood sweets for many years. I had forgotten how good they are. But that was just the beginning. At home we made no more than half a dozen recipes and I needed around fifty. Finding them was no problem although not all the recipes I tried were reliable.

The biggest surprise was how good *all* the home-made sweets tasted. Even sweets I had never much cared for like marshmallows and Turkish delight taste fresher and more interesting when newly made with straightforward ingredients. That, of course, is the crucial difference between home- and factory-made sweets. We cannot use the battery of chemical additives available to today's confectionery manufacturers and our sweets taste much the better for it.

Another surprise was to discover how many traditional sweets seem not to be made any more. I could not recall what flavour pink Edinburgh rock should be. The easiest way to check would have been to buy some but I could not find it anywhere in London. When I did track it down on its native soil it was not the rock I remembered. It was too smooth, not roughly ridged any more.

Boiled sweets are another endangered species. There may be pockets of bullseyes and humbugs left but you have to look for them, and twirly sticks of golden barley sugar might already be extinct.

Danger of another kind threatens chocolate's reputation. The weasel words to watch for are 'chocolate-flavoured' and 'chocolate-flavoured coating'. High quality chocolate has never been cheap and that is not likely to change. Although the variety and availability of very luxurious, often hand-dipped chocolates have never been greater, the choice of competitively priced chocolate-flavoured sweets and bars is growing too. Satisfying an expensive taste for good chocolates is one reason for making your own. It certainly saves money.

Best of all, of course, making sweets is fun and offers endless scope for invention.

# —1—
# Equipment, ingredients and measures

No special equipment is needed for successful sweet-making. For boiling syrups you will need a good pan with a heavy base which will distribute heat evenly and discourage sticking and burning. A straight-sided untinned copper pan with a pouring lip is designed especially for sugar boiling. A chef pâtissière in a good kitchen would use such a pan, but at home it would be a luxury.

Always use a pan which allows plenty of room for the boiling ingredients to foam up. Rich mixtures are in particular danger of boiling over in too small a pan.

For pulled sweets, which are made by pouring hot syrup on to a cold slab and working it as it cools to change the texture, sometimes literally by pulling it as it hardens, the ideal work surface is marble. A large metal baking sheet or any other smooth, heat-resistant surface will suffice. For making cooked fondant and Edinburgh rock, and other confections which require considerable manual effort, it should be firmly anchored.

Non-stick tins are a boon to toffee makers. They really do make turning it out easier. A useful size is 20 cm (8 in) square.

If the increasingly wide range of confectionery supplies available from specialist kitchen shops is any indication, sweet-making is becoming a very popular pastime indeed. A number now stock chocolate moulds, dipping forks, and even hardened rubber blocks for moulding dozens of fondants.

Woodnutt's of 97 Church Road, Hove, Sussex BN3 2BA, telephone (0273) 738840, is a particularly useful mail order supplier of couverture, the high quality chocolate used by professional confectioners. Woodnutt's also sells a full range of moulds and odd ingredients like liquid glucose and gum arabic powder which can be difficult to buy locally.

Other mail order suppliers of confectionery equipment include the following:

Divertimenti, 68 Marylebone Lane, London W1M 5FF. 01-935 0689.

David Mellor, 4 Sloane Square, London SW1W 8EE. 01-730 4259.

Elizabeth David, 46 Bourne Street, London SW1W 8JB. 01-730 3123.

Baker Smith (Cake Decorators) Limited, 65 The Street, Tongham, Farnham, Surrey GU10 1DE. (02518) 2984.

Mary Ford Cake Artistry Centre, 28–30 Southbourne Grove, Southbourne, Bournemouth BH6 3HA. (0202) 431001.

A sugar-boiling thermometer is useful, but by no means essential. Perhaps surprisingly, accurate temperature measurement, and then the ability to control quite low temperatures, is essential only for working with chocolate. The reason a thermometer is of limited use when making fudge, caramels and the like is that the butter, milk, syrup, honey and various other ingredients in these sweets in addition to the sugar, all act as interfering agents which alter the temperature at which the basic syrup will behave in a completely predictable way.

The texture of a sugar syrup once it has cooled – soft, chewy, brittle or any stage between – depends on the temperature to which it was boiled. The higher the temperature the more moisture is driven from the syrup and the harder the finished

Testing syrup – the soft ball stage. When rolled with the fingers the syrup will form a soft, sticky ball.

sweet. The temperature bands, their names and how to test for them are as follows.

**Soft ball**      112°C to 116°C (234°F to 240°F)
*Fondants*         Drop a small spoonful of syrup into cold
*Fudge*            or iced water. When rolled with the fingers
                   the syrup will form a soft, sticky ball.

**Firm ball**      118°C to 121°C (244°F to 250°F)
*Caramels*         Drop a small spoonful of syrup into cold or
                   iced water. When rolled with the fingers the
                   syrup will form a firm, but still rather sticky
                   ball which loses its shape quite quickly out of
                   the water.

**Hard ball**      121°C to 130°C (250°F to 266°F)
*Marshmallows*     Drop a small spoonful of syrup into cold
*Nougat*           or iced water. When rolled with the fingers
                   the syrup will quickly form a ball which,
                   though sticky, will hold its shape out of
                   water.

**Soft crack**     132°C to 143°C (270°F to 290°F)
*Toffees*          Drop a small spoonful of syrup into cold
*Butterscotch*     or iced water. Take it out and pull it. It will
                   separate into hard, pliable strands.

**Hard crack**     149°C to 154°C (300°F to 310°F)
*Fruit drops*      Drop a small spoonful of syrup into cold
*Toffee*           or iced water. Take it out and break
*Barley sugar*     it. It should snap easily and will not
*Bullseyes*        be sticky.

**Caramel**        160°C to 177°C (320°F to 350°F)
*Brittles*         Smell and colour are caramel's distin-
*Praline*          guishing features. The colour can vary from
                   pale honey gold to rich amber but should not
                   be darker or the caramel will be bitter rather
                   than sweet.

Perfectionists have the patience to note that dipping the base of a pan of boiling syrup into cold water will stop the temperature of the syrup rising higher. If it has not yet reached the required stage it can be put back on the heat to cook a little longer. At the higher temperatures an overcooked syrup cannot be rescued, so arresting cooking to test it is a wise precaution.

Working at temperatures like these demands special care for safety. Being methodical and organized and never hurrying are good safeguards against accidents. Never leave the handles of pans protruding from the top of the stove.

The best immediate treatment for burns, however trivial or severe, is to hold the burned area of skin under cold running water for a full ten minutes. This minimizes the damage caused by the accident. Then keep the burned area clean and dry, and seek medical attention if necessary.

**Notes for American and Australian users**

In America the 8-fl oz measuring cup is used. In Australia metric measures are now used in conjunction with the standard 250-ml measuring cup. The Imperial pint, used in Britain and Australia, is 20 fl oz, while the American pint is 16 fl oz. It is important to remember that the Australian tablespoon differs from both the British and American tablespoons; the table below gives a comparison. The British standard tablespoon, which has been used throughout this book, holds 15 ml, the American 14.2 ml, and the Australian 20 ml. A teaspoon holds approximately 5 ml in all three countries.

| British | American | Australian |
|---|---|---|
| 1 teaspoon | 1 teaspoon | 1 teaspoon |
| 1 tablespoon | 1 tablespoon | 1 tablespoon |
| 2 tablespoons | 3 tablespoons | 2 tablespoons |
| 3½ tablespoons | 4 tablespoons | 3 tablespoons |
| 4 tablespoons | 5 tablespoons | 3½ tablespoons |

**An Imperial/American guide to solid and liquid measures**

SOLID MEASURES

| IMPERIAL | AMERICAN |
|---|---|
| 1 lb butter or margarine | 2 cups |
| 1 lb granulated or caster sugar | 2 cups |
| 1 lb icing sugar | 3 cups |

LIQUID MEASURES

| IMPERIAL | AMERICAN |
|---|---|
| ¼ pint liquid | ⅔ cup liquid |
| ½ pint | 1¼ cups |
| ¾ pint | 2 cups |
| 1 pint | 2½ cups |
| 1½ pints | 3¾ cups |
| 2 pints | 5 cups (2½ pints) |

Note: when making any of the recipes in this book, only follow one set of measures as they are not interchangeable.

# —2—
# Cool sweets
# that need
# no cooking

Nuts, dried fruits like dates, apricots, prunes and raisins, and wild and garden flowers are appealing ingredients in every way and it takes little trouble to turn them into the finest confectionery. Sweets that need no cooking can be tackled safely by the smallest fingers, but there is nothing childish or unsophisticated about the results. Marzipan can be modelled into shapes as simple or ornate as your skills and style dictate, and uncooked fondant makes classically elegant peppermint creams. As for crystallized flowers, they are simply exquisite. They make almost heartbreakingly pretty decorations for sweets, cakes and ices.

---

Very strictly speaking, marzipan is a cooked paste of nuts (usually almonds) and sugar. But so many people now say marzipan when they mean an uncooked confection that the correct use is fast becoming a technical term.

Marzipan has been popular in England since Tudor times, and probably before. It was known then as marchpane, and for feasts and festivals was coloured and sometimes even gilded.

## · MARZIPAN ALLSORTS ·

*Makes about 900 g (2 lb)*

**450 g (1 lb) ground almonds, or a mixture of almonds with ground hazelnuts or pistachios**
**450 g (1 lb) icing sugar**
**2–3 egg whites, lightly beaten**
**a few drops almond essence**
**food colouring**

---

Put the ground nuts and sugar in a bowl and mix them well before stirring in egg white, a little at a time, until the mixture is damp enough to stick together and can be made into a ball.

Turn out the paste on to a cool surface and knead it lightly to make it smooth and firm. Work in a little almond essence as

16

you knead the marzipan. Be careful not to work the paste too much or allow it to become too warm; this would encourage the nut oil to leak out and make the marzipan greasy.

At this stage the marzipan is ready to use and can be stored for a month or more in the refrigerator wrapped in foil or a plastic bag.

To colour and shape marzipan, set it on a cool surface which has been dusted with icing sugar and knead in a few drops of the chosen food colouring. One batch of paste can be divided into a number of small pieces and each coloured a different shade. Then the marzipan can be modelled, like plasticine, with the fingers, or rolled out like pastry and cut into a variety of shapes.

For a change of taste and texture work small amounts of chopped nuts, candied fruit or finely grated zest of an orange, lemon or lime into the marzipan and cut it in simple shapes.

For more exciting-looking sweets, stripy squares or swirling pinwheels, roll out sheets of two or more different colours of marzipan. Cut the sheets into strips and stack or roll them into batons, sticking the layers together lightly with brushed on egg white. Then, using a sharp knife, slice each bar or roll of marzipan into individual sweets.

Marzipan allsorts are best left to dry in a cool, airy place for a few hours before being eaten. To store them, put in an airtight container and keep in a cool place.

# · STUFFED DATES ·

*Makes about 450 g (1 lb)*

**450 g (1 lb) dates, fresh or dried**
**170 g (6 oz) marzipan**
**caster sugar to coat (optional)**

Carefully remove the stones from the dates without spoiling the shape of the fruit. Slit each date along one long side and prise out the stone.

Roll teaspoonfuls of marzipan into fat sausage-shaped pieces which taper at each end. Stuff each date with one of these marzipan lozenges. Roll the dates in caster sugar, or leave them plain.

Store stuffed dates in an airtight container in a cool place.

*Toot* is the name for Persian, or rather Iranian, marzipan. Like many other Middle Eastern sweets it is perfumed with rosewater. In *Persian Cooking* (University Press of Virginia) Nesta Ramazani describes how the sweets are fashioned to look like white mulberries and how when narcissus are in bloom, handfuls of the flowers are buried in the almonds for several days to perfume them.

# · TOOT ·

*Makes about 450 g (1 lb)*

**340 g (12 oz) ground almonds**
**110 g (4 oz) icing sugar**
**rosewater**
**caster sugar to dredge**
**55 g (2 oz) slivered pistachio nuts**

Combine the ground almonds and icing sugar with enough rosewater to make a stiff paste.

Form the sweets into stubby rolls about half as long again as they are thick. Roll the sweets in caster sugar to coat them on all sides then place a sliver of green pistachio nut into one end to resemble a mulberry stem.

Store the sweets in an airtight container to prevent them drying.

As addicts of hazelnut and chocolate spreads have already discovered, the two flavours go particularly well together. The combination is equally successful in sweets.

# · CHAZELS ·

*Makes about 450 g (1 lb)*

225 g (8 oz) shelled hazelnuts
225 g (8 oz) icing sugar
4 tablespoons cocoa
1–2 egg whites, lightly beaten

Grind the hazelnuts finely in a coffee grinder or food processor and mix them with the icing sugar and cocoa. Stir in
enough of the egg white, adding a little at a time, to make a
stiff paste. Knead the paste lightly to make it smooth and firm.

Form the paste into balls and allow them to dry a little before
storing in an airtight container. The paste may also be rolled
out and cut into other shapes and left plain, or dredged in
sugar, drinking chocolate powder, or chopped hazelnuts.

Lightly toasting hazelnuts changes and enhances their
flavour. It also makes the skins very easy to rub off. Toasted
nuts can also be used in the last recipe to great effect. If you
cannot buy them ready toasted, spread shelled nuts on a
baking sheet and bake them in a preheated moderate oven
(160°C/325°F, gas mark 3) for about 15 minutes. Allow them to
cool, then tip them into a clean cloth and rub off the skins.
Grind them and make the sweets as described.

# · APRICOT BALLS ·

*Makes about 450 g (1 lb)*

225 g (8 oz) dried apricots
110 g (4 oz) seedless raisins
110 g (4 oz) stoned prunes or dates
1 teaspoon finely grated tangerine or orange zest (optional)
1 to 2 tablespoons runny honey
about 85 g (3 oz) granulated sugar

First mince together twice the apricots, raisins and prunes or dates (the finest blade of the mincer is best for this), or use a food processor to reduce the dried fruit to a very thick paste.

Now add the grated zest if you are using it, and work in just enough of the honey to glue the mixture together without making it sticky. The exact amount will depend on the dryness of the fruit, so add the honey cautiously a little at a time.

Form small spoonfuls of the mixture into balls by rolling them between your palms, then roll the balls in granulated sugar to coat them evenly.

Space out the sweets on a wire cooling rack and leave them to firm up and dry a little. After twelve hours or so the flavours will have blended together too and they will taste even better.

Any mixture of dried fruits can be combined to make your own variations of the recipe. Small amounts of ground spices like cinnamon or cloves are good additions too.

Peppermint creams are very easy to make. Just about the only mistake that will spoil them is adding too much peppermint, so add it a very little at a time. Oil of peppermint from chemist shops is very fierce indeed and a few drops will flavour a whole batch of sweets. Peppermint essence will not be quite as strong.

# · PEPPERMINT CREAMS ·

*Makes about 450 g (1 lb)*

**2 egg whites**
**450 g (1 lb) icing sugar**
**peppermint oil or essence to taste**

Whisk the egg whites until they are frothy. Sieve the icing sugar into a bowl and stir in enough of the egg white to make a good stiff paste. Add the peppermint a drop at a time, working each drop in thoroughly before adding another.

To make the peppermint creams really smooth and silky knead the mixture for five minutes before rolling it out on a flat surface which has been lightly sprinkled with sieved icing sugar.

The traditional shape for peppermint creams is flat and round. Roll the mixture to about 7 mm (¼ in) thick and cut out rounds using a small biscuit cutter or perhaps a glass or an eggcup. Alternatively make square peppermint creams or roll teaspoonfuls of the mixture into balls.

To dry the sweets, arrange them in one layer on a tray lined with greaseproof paper and leave for twenty-four hours in a warm, airy place. Turn them at least once. When they have formed a thin crust on the outside they are ready to eat. If they are to be packed, dry them for another twenty-four hours.

Peppermint creams are sometimes tinted very pale green with a few drops of green food colouring. Small mint leaves painted with egg white and dipped in caster sugar make a pretty decoration but only use them for sweets which will be eaten up quickly because they will become dry and dusty if left out and the decoration is too fragile for them to be packed in layers.

Always keep peppermint creams separate from other sweets. If you don't, everything in the box or tin will soon taste of mint too.

Lemon creams can be made from the same mixture as peppermint creams, differently flavoured of course. This is uncooked fondant and it does have the one disadvantage that it becomes dry and brittle very quickly. If the sweets are for a present or for a sale or fête then it is worth adding liquid glucose (available from chemists) or a little cream of tartar. Either of these will keep the creams softer for longer. Alternatively, cooked fondants, like rose or maple flavoured sweets (see pages 68–9), keep even better.

# · LEMON CREAMS ·

*Makes about 450 g (1 lb)*

**450 g (1 lb) icing sugar**
**¼ teaspoon cream of tartar**
**2 egg whites**
**lemon essence to taste**
**yellow food colouring**

Sift the icing sugar and cream of tartar together into a bowl. Whisk the egg whites until they are frothy and stir enough egg white into the sugar to make a stiff paste. Work in the lemon flavouring a drop at a time until the mixture tastes as lemony as you like and then add a few drops of yellow colouring. Fondants and creams are traditionally pale and pastel coloured.

Knead the mixture for five minutes to make it really smooth then roll it out on a flat surface which has been lightly sprinkled with sieved icing sugar.

Cut out squares, or rounds, or any shape you fancy and lay the lemon creams out to dry in one layer on a tray lined with greaseproof paper. Turn them during drying. After twenty-four hours in a warm, airy place they should have formed a thin crust. Store them in a dry place.

When small amounts of condensed milk are needed, as in this recipe for chocolate refrigerator fudge, buying it in a re-sealable tube may be more economical than opening a tin.

# · CHOCOLATE REFRIGERATOR · FUDGE

*Makes about 1.35 kg (3 lb)*

**170 g (6 oz) butter, unsalted or slightly salted**
**340 g (12 oz) plain chocolate**
**680 g (1½ lb) caster sugar**
**1 large egg**
**4 tablespoons sweetened condensed milk**
**2 teaspoons vanilla essence**
**110 g (4 oz) chopped glacé cherries, raisins or walnuts (optional)**

Lightly butter a straight-sided tin measuring about 20 by 30 cm (8 by 12 in).

Put the butter and the chocolate, broken into squares, into a bowl and set it over a pan or bowl of very hot water. As the chocolate only has to melt there is no need to have this on or near the stove. Stir the mixture until it has melted into a smooth paste.

In a large bowl mix the caster sugar with the egg, condensed milk and vanilla essence then stir in every drop of the melted chocolate. Now add the cherries, raisins or walnuts if you are using them. Stir the mixture until it is well blended then turn it into the prepared tin and smooth the top flat.

Chill the fudge in the fridge for two hours or more before

cutting it into neat squares. It will taste even better after a day or two than it does on the day it is made.

Sugared rose petals, candied violets, crystallized pinks – real flowers preserved in sugar are the prettiest and most romantic of all confections. Use these fragile, scented blossoms to decorate ices, chocolates or cakes.

If you do not have a garden, or want to make crystallized flowers in winter, freesias from a florist are one possible choice.

Traditionally two substances have been used to coat the petals before they are sprinkled with sugar – gum arabic or egg white. Both do the job very well but I would give gum arabic the edge because it is dissolved in rose water and so adds to rather than detracts from the scent of the blossoms.

By no means all flowers are edible so don't go eating any flower not mentioned here without checking carefully with a reliable source to make sure it is not poisonous. The following list offers plenty of choice through a long season: primroses, violets, apple blossom, clove-gilly flowers (wallflowers), marigolds, nasturtiums, geraniums, pinks, carnations, lobelia, roses, jasmine, mimosa, lilac, borage, orange blossom and freesias. The leaves of well-known herbs like thyme, basil, rosemary and sage can be candied too, and so, of course, can their flowers.

OPPOSITE *Sweets, from left: peppermint creams with crystallized mint leaves, stuffed dates, and marzipan allsorts.*

OVERLEAF *Sweets, from left: candied popcorn, Edinburgh rock, rich chocolate truffles, assorted chocolates, toffee bars and barley sugar, and chocolate cups.*

# · CRYSTALLIZED FLOWERS ·

*Makes plenty, say 50 rose petals*

**1 teaspoon gum arabic OR 1 egg white**
**2 teaspoons rosewater (if using gum arabic)**
**225 g (8 oz) caster sugar**
**fresh, dry flowers in perfect condition**

Put the gum arabic and rosewater into a very small dish and stir until the resin has dissolved completely, or break up the egg white with a fork but do not make it too frothy.

Spread some of the caster sugar on a plate and put some of the remainder in a small sieve or coffee strainer.

If you are candying roses or other fairly large flowers, separate them into petals and nip off the white heel at the base of each petal. Very small flowers, individual lilac flowers, lobelia, violets and primroses can be crystallized whole.

Painting a small flower with egg-white.

OPPOSITE *Sweets, from top: toffee apples, candied popcorn, yellowman, peanut brittle, pecan candies, and nut clusters.*

Using a small, soft brush paint each petal or flower sparingly front and back with gum or egg white. Then lay the petals or flowers on the plate of sugar and sprinkle more sugar over them. It is best to work with one petal or flower at a time, sugaring each immediately it has been painted. Put the sugared flowers on clean paper laid on baking trays and dry them in an airing cupboard or barely warm oven for twenty-four hours. Turn the flowers several times in the first three or four hours if you can to let the air dry them on all sides. Once they are very dry and brittle they can be stored in airtight containers and keep well for many months.

# —3—
# Hard-boiled sweets

Have you read any good sweet wrappers lately? I confess I had not until I was trying to find sweets which fitted the diet of someone forbidden a number of common food additives, including some of the most widely used colourings and emulsifiers. It was impossible. Even the most straightforward boiled sweets, jellies, gums and pastilles included, when their ingredients were listed at all, all kinds of unexpected substances.

Now there probably was not an additive harmful to most people in any of these bought sweets, but I have come to like home-made sweets more and more because I know exactly what has gone into them. Fruit from the garden or market can be used to flavour fruit drops and lolliberrypops. Barley sugar made with sugar and fresh lemons is as pure and golden as it looks. And to flavour humbugs with peppermint and bullseyes with cloves there is a choice of natural extracts, the real essential oils, as well as manufactured essences.

---

Fruit drops and lollipops are the easiest of all boiled sweets to make at home. Sharp fruits with plenty of taste like raspberries, blackcurrants or redcurrants give the finest natural flavours.

## · LOLLIBERRYPOPS ·

*Makes about 450 g (1 lb)*

450 g (1 lb) fresh or frozen raspberries, strawberries, blackcurrants or redcurrants
450 g (1 lb) granulated sugar
1 tablespoon liquid glucose

---

Put the fruit in a medium-sized pan and heat it, covered, very gently until the juices begin to run. Uncover and stir once or twice. Do not boil or the juice will evaporate.

Strain the juice through a fine sieve. Discard the fruit pulp

28

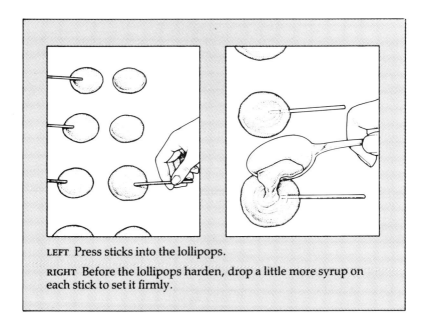

**LEFT** Press sticks into the lollipops.

**RIGHT** Before the lollipops harden, drop a little more syrup on each stick to set it firmly.

or use it to flavour yogurt or muesli. There should be about 150 ml (¼ pt) of pure fruit juice.

Put the juice back in the pan with the sugar and glucose. Heat gently until the sugar has dissolved completely, using a pastry brush dipped in water to wash down any crystals which stick to the sides of the pan. Bring the syrup to the boil and boil it fast until it reaches the hard crack stage (149°C/300°F).

Spoon small puddles of the syrup on to an oiled heat-resistant surface (marble is best or a baking sheet). Press sticks into the lollipops and, before they harden, drop a little more syrup on each stick to set it firmly.

When the scarlet or purple lolliberrypops are hard and brittle, prise them off the work surface with a palette knife or slice. Wrap them in cellophane or greaseproof paper and store in an airtight container.

Clear concentrated fruit drinks, such as lime or black-currant, can also be used to make sparkling transparent sweets. Use about 150 ml (¼ pt) to every 450 g (1 lb) of sugar.

# · REAL FRUIT DROPS ·

*Makes about 450 g (1 lb)*

**150 ml (¼ pt) freshly squeezed lemon or lime juice, or soft fruit
juice (see previous recipe)
450 g (1 lb) granulated sugar
1 tablespoon liquid glucose**

Put the juice into a medium-sized pan with the sugar and
glucose. Heat together gently until the sugar has dissolved
completely, and wash down any sugar crystals from the sides
of the pan with a pastry brush dipped in cold water.

Raise the heat and boil the syrup to the hard crack stage
(149°C/300°F), then immediately dip the base of the pan into
cold water to stop the temperature of the sugar rising higher.

Drop teaspoonfuls of the syrup on to an oiled heat-resistant
surface and allow them to cool completely. Wrap the fruit
drops individually in clear cellophane before storing in an
airtight container.

# · BUTTERSCOTCH ·

*Makes about 450 g (1 lb)*

**450 g (1 lb) granulated sugar
150 ml (¼ pt) water
¼ teaspoon cream of tartar
85 g (3 oz) butter, diced
½ teaspoon vanilla essence**

Butter a 20-cm (8-in) square tin and set it aside.

Put the sugar and water in a medium-sized pan and heat
gently until the sugar has dissolved completely. Wash down
any sugar crystals from the sides of the pan with a pastry
brush dipped in cold water. Stir in the cream of tartar then,
without stirring more, boil the syrup to the soft ball stage
(116°C/240°F). Take the pan off the heat.

Off the heat, stir in the butter, then boil the syrup again, this time to the soft crack stage (143°C/290°F). Stir in the vanilla essence and pour the butterscotch into its prepared tin.

When the butterscotch is beginning to firm, use an oiled knife to mark it into squares, then leave it to set hard. Break it into the squares marked, and wrap it in traditional foil or another wrapping. Butterscotch keeps well in an airtight container.

Twisted sticks of golden barley sugar are the kind of really old-fashioned sweets that have almost disappeared from shops. Yet at the height of their popularity they were much harder work to make than they are today.

In *Gunter's Confectioner's Oracle* published in 1830, William Gunter describes the work necessary to make the loaf sugar of the day suitable for 'works in caramel or barley sugar'. To achieve 'fine clarification' he instructs the cook to 'break up a twelve-pound loaf of fine sugar, and put it in a vessel with two quarts and half-a-pint of water; mix three whites of eggs with a pound and a quarter of ivory black.* Put all together on a slow fire, so that the sugar does not boil (cold water, in small quantities, prevents ebullition): and when the dissolution is complete, pass the mass frequently through a bag of flannel. The product will be at length of exquisite transparency and whiteness.'

The stages of sugar boiling were differently named too in the pompous Mr Gunter's day. After *thread* came *the pearl* followed by *the blow, the feather, the ball, the crack* and *the caramel*. His test for *the blow* was as follows: 'sparkling and bubbling created by blowing through the holes of the skimmer, discover the blow.'

Here then is Mr Gunter's recipe for barley sugar. 'Add some drops of acid (lemon juice) while the sugar is at the crack, take it off the fire, and instantly plunge the lower part of the pan in a dish of cold water.

* Ivory black, literally calcined ivory, was used as a clarifying agent much as charcoal is used as a filter today.

'Pour it on a marble table prepared with oil, and, dividing the barley sugar into portions, roll it out with your hand; add any essence you think proper, but always in moderation, or delicacy of flavour will be destroyed.'

Mr Gunter then added, and the italics are his: '*Twisted* sugar is somewhat *vulgar* as an article'. Is it now? I think twirly sticks of barley sugar are a great pleasure.

# · BARLEY SUGAR ·

*Makes about 450 g (1 lb)*

**450 g (1 lb) granulated sugar**
**150 ml (¼ pt) water**
**finely pared zest of ½ lemon**
**¼ teaspoon cream of tartar**
**2 tablespoons fresh lemon juice**

Generously smear with oil a large marble slab or heat-resistant board or work surface.

Put the sugar in a medium-sized pan with the water and set it on a low heat until the sugar has dissolved completely. Wash down any sugar crystals from the sides of the pan with a pastry brush dipped in cold water.

Drop the lemon zest into the syrup and stir in the cream of tartar. Bring it to the boil and cook the syrup to the soft ball stage (116°C/240°F). Stir in the lemon juice and continue cooking until the syrup reaches the hard crack stage (154°C/310°F). Take the pan off the heat and dip the base briefly in cold water to stop the syrup bubbling quickly. Pour it on to the oiled work surface.

Allow the syrup to cool a little more until it stiffens at the edges and begins to form a skin. Use an oiled palette knife or slice to lift one edge of the hardening pool of syrup and fold it into the centre. Fold the opposite edge in the same way.

Now, working quickly, use oiled scissors to cut the barley sugar into narrow strips. Immediately twist each strip into a curly stick, and set it aside to harden completely. If the last of

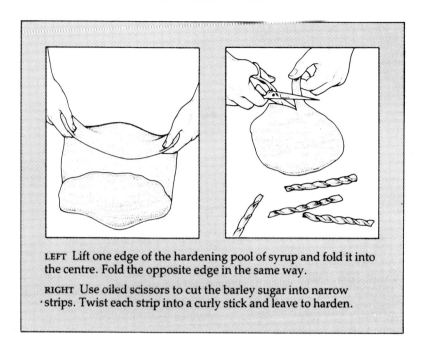

**LEFT** Lift one edge of the hardening pool of syrup and fold it into the centre. Fold the opposite edge in the same way.

**RIGHT** Use oiled scissors to cut the barley sugar into narrow ·strips. Twist each strip into a curly stick and leave to harden.

the candy hardens before it has been shaped just break it into small pieces to eat as sweets.

Wrap each barley sugar piece individually in clear cellophane and store in an airtight container.

Vinegar candy is one of the easiest to make of the pulled sugar sweets. Its sweet-sour taste, reminiscent of pickle, has long been popular in the United States where it is a favourite old-fashioned candy to make at home.

# · VINEGAR CANDY ·

*Makes about 450 g (1 lb)*

**450 g (1 lb) golden granulated sugar**
**150 ml (¼ pt) cider vinegar**

Generously oil a marble slab or suitable heat-resistant surface.

Put the sugar in a medium-sized pan with the vinegar and heat gently until the sugar has dissolved completely. Wash down any crystals from the sides of the pan with a pastry brush dipped in cold water. Raise the heat and boil the syrup to the soft crack stage (140°C/284°F). Immediately pour the syrup on to the prepared surface. To help it cool evenly, turn the sides to the middle using an oiled palette knife.

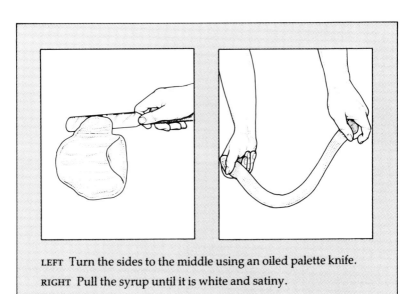

LEFT Turn the sides to the middle using an oiled palette knife.
RIGHT Pull the syrup until it is white and satiny.

When it is cool enough to handle, oil your hands and pull the syrup until it is white and satiny. Form it into a rope and cut into short lengths with oiled scissors. Store the sweets in an airtight container between sheets of greaseproof paper, or individually wrapped.

## · TOFFEE BARS ·

*Makes about 570 g (1¼ lb)*

**450 g (1 lb) golden granulated sugar**
**110 g (4 oz) butter**
**150 ml (¼ pt) water**
**1 tablespoon fresh lemon juice**

Generously butter or oil a 20-cm (8-in) square tin.

Put the sugar in a medium-sized saucepan with the butter, water and lemon juice. Heat slowly, stirring, until the sugar has dissolved completely. Wash down any sugar crystals from the sides of the pan with a pastry brush dipped in cold water. Raise the heat and boil the syrup to the soft crack stage

35

(140°C/284°F). Immediately pour the syrup into the prepared tin and leave it to cool a little.

While it is still warm, use an oiled knife to score the toffee deeply into bars about 1.25 cm (½ in) wide by 7.5 cm (3 in) long. When the toffee is cold and brittle, break it along the score marks and wrap the bars individually before storing them in an airtight container.

# · RUM BUTTER DROPS ·

*Makes about 600 g (1¼ lb)*

450 g (1 lb) granulated sugar
110 g (4 oz) butter
150 ml (¼ pt) water
½ teaspoon rum essence

Oil or butter a smooth marble, metal or enamelled surface.

Put the sugar, butter and water in a heavy pan and heat gently together until the sugar has melted completely. Wash down any sugar crystals from the sides of the pan with a pastry brush dipped in cold water.

Bring the syrup to the boil and boil it briskly to the soft crack stage (140°C/284°F). Quickly stir in the essence and pour the syrup into small pools on the prepared surface. Use a spoon to measure out the syrup if this is easier – it depends on your pan. Leave the drops to harden and when they are quite cold wrap them individually before storing them in an airtight container.

Two separate syrups are needed to make black and white striped peppermint humbugs. First there is a clear syrup which is pulled until it is white and satiny, and then a second syrup coloured with black food colouring. (Dark brown or red will do if you cannot find black.) But because the two colours must be worked together both syrups must be made at the same time, otherwise one will have set hard before the second is ready.

# · HUMBUGS ·

*Makes about 450 g (1 lb)*

**570 g (1¼ lb) granulated sugar**
**150 ml (¼ pt) water**
**1 tablespoon liquid glucose**
**oil of peppermint or peppermint essence**
**black, brown or red food colouring**

Generously oil a large marble slab or metal surface. Divide the sugar, water and glucose equally between two saucepans and heat gently until the sugar has dissolved completely. Wash down any crystals from the sides of the pans with a pastry brush dipped in cold water. Stir peppermint flavouring into both syrups, and food colouring into one only. Raise the heat and boil the syrups to the hard crack stage (149°C/300°F). Immediately dip the base of the pans in cold water to stop the temperature rising higher.

Pour the syrups into separate pools on the prepared surface. Using an oiled palette knife, turn the sides into the middle of the coloured syrup.

As soon as the uncoloured syrup is cool enough to handle, oil your hands and gather it into a sausage shape (see page 38). Use both hands to pull the sausage into a rope and double it back into a sausage shape several times. Continue pulling the syrup until it becomes white and satiny, then flatten it out into a rough rectangle.

Gather up the coloured syrup and form it into a sausage the same length as the white candy. Roll up the coloured piece inside the white one, then pull and twist the combination sausage a few times to make a stripy rope. Don't overdo the pulling and twisting at this stage or the stripes will disappear.

Now, using oiled scissors, cut the rope into short lengths, giving it a half turn between every cut to produce traditionally

37

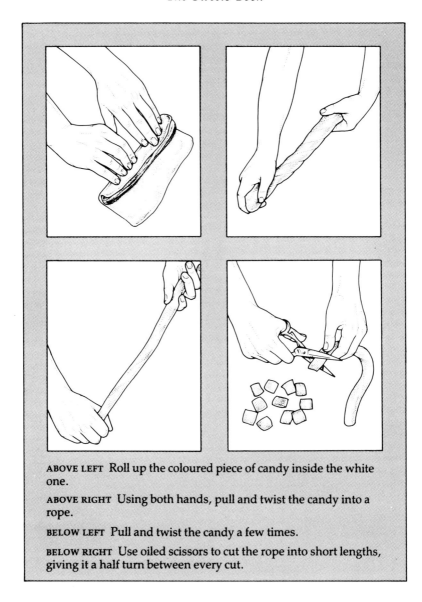

**ABOVE LEFT** Roll up the coloured piece of candy inside the white one.

**ABOVE RIGHT** Using both hands, pull and twist the candy into a rope.

**BELOW LEFT** Pull and twist the candy a few times.

**BELOW RIGHT** Use oiled scissors to cut the rope into short lengths, giving it a half turn between every cut.

triangular humbugs. When the sweets are cold and hard, wrap them in cellophane or store them loose but separated by sheets of greaseproof paper in an airtight container.

The procedure for making clove balls is almost identical to the humbug method with one extra step, rolling the cut sweets into small balls. The humbug ingredients can be similarly used to make peppermint bullseyes.

# · CLOVE BALLS ·

*Makes about 450 g (1 lb)*

**570 g (1¼ lb) granulated sugar**
**150 ml (¼ pt) water**
**1 tablespoon liquid glucose**
**oil of cloves or clove essence**
**red food colouring**

Generously oil a large marble slab or metal surface.

Divide the sugar, water and glucose between two saucepans and heat gently until the sugar has dissolved completely. Wash down any crystals from the sides of the pans with a pastry brush dipped in cold water. Stir clove flavouring into both syrups, and red colouring into one only. Raise the heat then boil the syrups to the hard crack stage (149°C/300°F). Immediately dip the base of the pans into cold water to stop the temperature of the syrups rising higher.

Pour the syrups into separate pools on the prepared surface. Using an oiled palette knife, turn the sides to the middle of the coloured syrup.

As soon as the uncoloured syrup is cool enough to handle, oil your hands and gather it into a sausage shape. Use both hands to pull the sausage into a rope and double it back into a sausage shape several times. Continue pulling the syrup until it becomes white and satiny, then flatten it out into a rough rectangle.

Gather up the coloured syrup and form it into a sausage the same length as the white candy. Roll up the coloured piece inside the white one, then pull and twist the combination sausage a few times to make a stripy rope.

Use scissors with oiled blades to cut the rope into short

lengths, and oiled hands to roll each piece into a ball.

The finished sweets can be individually wrapped in cellophane and stored in an airtight container. Unwrapped sweets are best separated by layers of greaseproof paper.

# —4—
# Chewy sweets and stickjaw

Toffees, nougats and other chewy sweets have an appeal all of their own. Stickjaw was the nineteenth-century slang name for sweets of this kind. The use of this splendidly graphic expression was never confined to any particular variety of toffee, so may be freely applied to every kind. It is too good a colloquialism to die.

---

Treacle toffee is the home-made sweet I remember best from my childhood because it was one of the most useful and popular when white sugar was strictly rationed during and for a surprisingly long time after the Second World War. Sometimes it was very chewy and sometimes almost brittle. That choice is still yours – it just depends on whether you boil it to hard ball, soft crack or right up to hard crack – and they are all delicious.

## · TREACLE TOFFEE ·

*Makes about 680 g (1½ lb)*

**110 g (4 oz) salted butter**
**450 g (1 lb) demerara or light muscovado sugar**
**300 ml (½ pt) molasses or black treacle**

---

Generously butter a non-stick tin measuring approximately 20 cm (8 in) square, or line a plain tin with buttered grease-proof paper.

Put the remaining butter, the sugar and molasses into a medium-sized pan and heat very slowly together until the sugar has dissolved completely. Wash down any sugar crystals from the sides of the pan with a pastry brush dipped in cold water. Then boil the syrup without stirring it, until it reaches soft crack (138°C/280°F), and pour it immediately into the prepared tin.

As this toffee will set hard it is a good idea to mark it out into squares as soon as it begins to set – use an oiled knife and a ruler – and to go over the markings at least once more before it is quite hard otherwise it will not break into neat pieces. If it is allowed to harden without being scored then it can only be cracked into jagged pieces like pot shards. (They taste just as good of course.)

Treacle toffee is traditionally wrapped in greaseproof paper. Sparkly cellophane looks more festive if the toffee is for sale or for a present.

Make your own vanilla scented sugar for use in toffees and fudge by putting one or two whole vanilla pods in a jar of sugar and leaving it, tightly closed, for a week or more. It keeps indefinitely and gives an even better flavour than adding vanilla essence at the end of cooking.

## · VANILLA CARAMELS ·

*Makes about 400 g (14 oz)*

**45 g (1½ oz) salted butter**
**225 g (8 oz) plain or vanilla-flavoured granulated sugar**
**250 ml (8 fl oz) double cream**
**4 tablespoons runny honey**
**1–2 teaspoons vanilla essence (optional)**

Generously butter a non-stick tin measuring approximately 20 cm (8 in) square, or line a plain tin with buttered grease-proof paper.

Put the remaining butter, sugar, cream and honey into a medium-sized pan and place over a moderate heat. Stir occasionally until the sugar has dissolved completely and wash down any sugar crystals on the sides of the pan with a pastry brush dipped in cold water. Then boil the mixture, stirring it occasionally to prevent sticking, until it reaches the hard ball stage (121°C/250°F). Stir in the essence if you are using it and pour the syrup into the prepared tin.

When it has cooled and is firm turn it out on to a cutting surface and use an oiled knife to cut the block into neat squares. Wrap them individually in cellophane or greaseproof paper and store in an airtight container.

# · NUTTY TOFFEES ·

*Makes about 450 g (1 lb)*

**55 g (2 oz) salted butter**
**340 g (12 oz) soft brown sugar**
**300 ml (½ pt) double cream**
**1 teaspoon vanilla essence**
**110 g (4 oz) chopped hazels, walnuts or almonds**

Generously oil or butter a non-stick tin measuring approximately 20 cm (8 in) square.

Put the butter, sugar and cream into a heavy pan and heat slowly until the sugar has dissolved completely. Wash down any sugar crystals from the sides of the pan with a pastry brush dipped in cold water.

Raise the heat and boil the syrup, stirring occasionally to stop it catching, until it reaches the hard ball stage (121°C/250°F). At once stir in the essence and nuts and pour the toffee into the prepared tin.

When the slab has cooled and firmed, but before it is quite cold, turn it on to a board and use a heavy, oiled knife to cut it into neat rectangles. Wrap the sweets individually in cellophane or greaseproof paper before storing them in an airtight container.

# · CHOCOLATE CARAMELS ·

*Makes about 450 g (1 lb)*

55 g (2 oz) salted butter
120 ml (4 fl oz) sweetened condensed milk
120 ml (4 fl oz) golden syrup
225 g (8 oz) granulated sugar
55 g (2 oz) cocoa powder
1 teaspoon vanilla essence

Generously butter a non-stick tin measuring 20 cm (8 in) square or line a plain tin with buttered greaseproof paper.

Put the remaining butter in a medium-sized pan with the condensed milk, golden syrup and sugar and heat the mixture slowly until the sugar has dissolved completely. Wash down any sugar crystals from the sides of the pan with a pastry brush dipped in cold water.

Now raise the heat and as soon as the syrup reaches boiling point, stir in the cocoa powder. Continue boiling it without further stirring until it reaches the hard ball stage (121°C/ 250°F). Stir in the vanilla essence and pour the syrup immediately into the prepared tin.

When the block has cooled and firmed, turn it on to a cutting surface and use an oiled knife to cut it into squares or batons. Wrap them individually and store in an airtight tin.

Vary the basic recipe by stirring 55 g (2 oz) each of nuts and raisins into the toffee at the same time as the essence, or by dipping each caramel in melted chocolate (see pages 86–7).


Home-made honey nougat, densely packed with toasted nuts, is one of the joys of sweet-making. It is a two-man, woman or child job unless you have an electric whisk to cope with the beating stage.

As well as elbow grease you will need a couple of sheets of rice paper, a board to weigh down the nougat as it sets, and some weights. Edible rice paper can be found in all sorts of shops from stationers to supermarkets and specialist cookery suppliers.

# · HONEY NOUGAT ·

*Makes about 570 g (1¼ lb)*

**225 g (8 oz) shelled hazelnuts**
**175 ml (6 fl oz) honey**
**225 g (8 oz) granulated sugar**
**6 tablespoons water**
**1 egg white, stiffly beaten**

To bring out the flavour of the hazelnuts and to skin them easily, spread them on a baking sheet and roast in a preheated moderate oven (160°C/325°F, gas mark 3) for about 15 minutes, or until the centres are a pale biscuit colour. Cool the nuts a little then tip them on to a clean dry cloth and rub off their skins. Keep them warm until needed.

Measure the honey into a jug and set it in a bowl of hot water to warm.

Put the sugar and water in a saucepan and cook over a low heat until the sugar has dissolved completely. Then without stirring, cook the syrup to the soft crack stage (138°C/280°F). Stir in the honey, then continue cooking until the temperature rises to soft crack again. Immediately remove the saucepan from the heat.

Now pour the syrup slowly into the stiffly beaten egg white, whisking constantly until the foam begins to thicken, then becomes stiff. To make it stiffen well it may be necessary to stand the bowl over a pan of boiling water and whisk over this additional heat. Fold in the warm nuts and spoon the nougat on to a baking sheet lined with rice paper. Spread it to a depth of about 1.25 cm (½ in) and top it with another sheet of rice paper. Cover this with a board, weight it well with books, tins or bricks and leave to set overnight.

Next day, use a large, heavy knife to cut the nougat into bars or squares. They can be wrapped in cellophane or greaseproof paper and keep well for several weeks stored in an airtight tin.

Nougat noir, or black nougat, is not really a nougat at all but a nutty brittle made with honey. It is a speciality of Provence in the south of France and is served as one of the thirteen traditional desserts offered at the Christmas meal.

# · NOUGAT NOIR ·

*Makes about 450 g (1 lb)*

**110 g (4 oz) granulated sugar**
**6 tablespoons runny honey**
**1 tablespoon orange flower water**
**225 g (8 oz) blanched almonds**

Put all the ingredients into a heavy saucepan and heat slowly, stirring often, until the sugar melts. Now boil the mixture slowly until the nuts and syrup both turn a warm, golden brown.

Pour the mixture on to a baking sheet or tin lined with rice paper and put another sheet of rice paper on top. There is no need to weight this mixture down. Leave it to cool and when quite cold break into bite-sized pieces.

How did the sweet called divinity get its name, I wonder? Like fudge, it seems that this is an American rather than a British invention, and it appears in almost every American cook book. Was it made for so many church bazaars and Sunday school picnics that it was named for its impeccable clerical credentials? Or could it be simply that it tastes divine?

Divinity is like soft nougat, melting and chewy at the same time. Instead of being set in a block though, divinity is spooned out in little bite-sized heaps which can be arranged in individual paper cases when they are dry.

# · CHERRY DIVINITY ·

*Makes about 680 g (1½ lb)*

450 g (1 lb) granulated sugar
4 tablespoons liquid glucose
150 ml (¼ pt) water
2 egg whites, stiffly beaten
1 teaspoon vanilla essence
225 g (8 oz) glacé cherries, cut in rings

Put the sugar, glucose and water into a medium-sized pan and heat slowly until the sugar has dissolved completely. Wash down any sugar crystals from the sides of the pan with a pastry brush dipped in cold water. Bring the syrup to the boil and cook until it reaches the hard ball stage (130°C/266°F).

Now whisk the syrup into the stiffly beaten egg whites in a steady stream. Continue beating until all the syrup has been used up and the meringue loses its shine and becomes stiff. Beat in the vanilla essence and fold in the sliced cherries.

Drop teaspoonfuls of the mixture on to sheets lined with greaseproof paper and leave them to cool and dry. Divinity is best eaten on the same day it is made.

Candied peel is a standby of the Christmas storecupboard and when fresh and well made it is a more appealing commodity than those little tubs of chopped peel sold in the supermarket. Recipes for candying fruit go back a long way. Mrs Mary Eales, who was confectioner to Queen Anne, recorded her recipes in a book published in 1718. Her instructions for making quince chips differ remarkably little from the modern candied peel recipe which follows it here.

**To make quince chips from *Mrs Mary Eales's Recipes***
'Pare the Quinces, and slice them into Water; put them into boiling Water; let them boil fast 'till they are very tender, but not so soft as to break them: Take them out with a skimmer,

lay them on a sieve 'till they are well drain'd, and have ready a very thick Syrup of clarify'd Sugar; put them into as much as will cover them, then boil them 'till they are very clear, and the next Day scald them; and if you see they want Syrup, put in a Pint more, but let it be very thick: Scald them twice more, then lay them in Earthen Plates in a Stove, sift them well with Sugar: Turn them and sift them 'till they are dry.'

Oranges, grapefruit and lemon are the most suitable citrus peels for candying, but resist the temptation to make a mixed batch. Their distinctive flavours are best captured separately. As well as being an ingredient in rich fruit cakes and puddings, candied peel can be eaten as a sweetmeat. Dipped in dark chocolate, orange peel makes one of the most sophisticated sweets to serve with coffee and liqueurs.

# · CANDIED PEEL ·

*Makes about 900 g (2 lb)*

**6 large lemons, or 5 large oranges, or 3 grapefruit**
**680 g (1½ lb) granulated sugar**
**250 ml (8 fl oz) water**

Quarter the fruit, scoop out the pulp but leave the white pith on the zest. Slice the skins into narrow strips.

To tenderize the peel and to soften the flavour of its bitter oils it must be boiled in several changes of water. Either soak it in cold water for several days before boiling it once till tender, or give it repeated boilings in fresh batches of water.

Combine the sugar and water in a heavy pan and heat slowly until the sugar has dissolved completely. Boil the syrup for five minutes before adding the peel. Simmer the peel in the syrup for about three-quarters of an hour then drain and dry it overnight on a wire rack.

Leave the peel in a warm, dry place until it has dried completely and lost its stickiness (this may take several days).

It can then be stored in an airtight container, or rolled in sugar or dipped in dark chocolate to eat as sweets.

# —5—
# Crunchy sweets

I n Scotland all confectionery is called sweeties so there is not the same confusion as there is in England where a sweet can be both a sweetmeat and a pudding.

Sweetie Sandy was the nickname given to Alexander Ferguson, founder of the firm which first made Edinburgh rock. He was born in 1798 in Perthshire and his father took a dim view of the boy's sweet-making games. Nonetheless, young Sandy trained as a confectioner and went on to found the firm which made its name and his fortune with Edinburgh rock. The discovery of the now world famous sweet is said to have been an accident. The story goes that when an inexplicably overlooked batch of candy was rediscovered it had become crumbly and fragile. Thank goodness someone was curious or greedy enough to taste it.

The unusual feature of making Edinburgh rock is still that once it has been shaped it is deliberately left out in a warm room, instead of being packed away immediately in an airtight tin. It is exposed to the air for about twenty-four hours, during which time the granulation process which begins with pulling the cooked sugar continues, and the rock becomes friable.

Traditionally Edinburgh rock comes in four colours, each of which has its own flavour. White is vanilla, pink is raspberry, yellow is lemon and beige, best of all, tastes of ginger.

# · EDINBURGH ROCK ·

*Makes about 450 g (1 lb)*

**450 g (1 lb) granulated sugar**
**300 ml (½ pt) water**
**¼ teaspoon cream of tartar**
**vanilla, raspberry, lemon or ginger essence**
**pink, yellow or brown food colouring**

Butter or oil a marble slab or heat-resistant surface.
Put the sugar and water in a heavy pan and heat gently until

the sugar has dissolved completely. Wash any sugar crystals down the sides of the pan with a pastry brush dipped in cold water. Then stir in the cream of tartar, raise the heat and boil the syrup to the hard ball stage (121°C/250°F).

Immediately pour the syrup on to the prepared surface. Allow it to cool a little then, using an oiled palette knife, lift the edges into the centre.

When the syrup is cool enough to handle, quickly knead in the chosen colouring and flavouring. The colours should always be pastel when the rock is ready. Now begin pulling the syrup, without twisting it, repeating the action until it loses its sheen and becomes dull.

Pull the rope of sugar out to the thickness you like (1.5 cm, just over ½ in, is ideal) and cut it into 10-cm/4-in lengths.

Lay out the rock on sheets of greaseproof paper and leave in a warm room for twenty-four hours before packing it.

Yellowman is the traditional name for honeycomb toffee which is still sold at country fairs in Northern Ireland. Its dense, bubbly texture is produced by adding bicarbonate of soda to hot syrup. It foams up hugely and instantly so be sure to use a big enough pan. In old versions of the recipe the toffee was pulled as well, but this is seldom done today.

Yellowman made with molasses instead of golden syrup is called blackman – that's traditional too.

# · YELLOWMAN ·

*Makes about 450 g (1 lb)*

55 g (2 oz) butter
225 g (8 oz) demerara sugar
175 ml (6 fl oz) golden syrup
1 tablespoon vinegar
2 teaspoons bicarbonate of soda

Generously butter a tin about 20 cm (8 in) square.

Put the remaining butter in a fairly large heavy saucepan over a low heat. When it has melted, add the sugar, syrup and vinegar. Heat gently until the sugar has dissolved completely then, without stirring it, boil the syrup to the hard crack stage (149°C/300°F). Immediately remove the pan from the heat and stir in the bicarbonate of soda. As soon as the mixture foams up stir it again and pour at once into the prepared tin.

When it is cool, mark into squares or bars and when quite cold, cut it up. Store yellowman in an airtight tin.

Peanut brittle is nicest made with peanuts which have been lightly roasted to bring out their flavour. Salted peanuts will not do.

The most straightforward way of making peanut brittle, putting the shelled nuts and sugar in a pan and heating them together until the sugar melts to an even caramel, calls for very careful heat control and a very good pan. The slow but sure method of the following recipe will be easier for beginners.

# · PEANUT BRITTLE ·

*Makes about 680 g (1½ lb)*

340 g (12 oz) fresh shelled peanuts
340 g (12 oz) golden granulated sugar
120 ml (4 fl oz) water

Generously oil or butter a marble slab or metal baking sheet.

Spread the nuts on a baking tray and roast them in a preheated moderate oven (160°C/325°F, gas mark 3) for about 10 minutes. Cool slightly then turn them on to a cloth and rub off their skins. Keep the nuts warm.

Put the sugar and water in a heavy pan and heat gently until the sugar has dissolved completely. Wash down any crystals on the sides of the pan with a pastry brush dipped in water. Raise the heat and boil the syrup hard to a light caramel (160°C/320°F). Quickly stir in the warm nuts and pour the mixture on to the prepared surface. When the syrup is cool enough to handle, pull it out quite thinly. When it has set hard, break the brittle into irregular pieces and store in an airtight container.

The technique for making sesame snaps is very similar to the method used for making brittle. Ideally the syrup will run thinly over the prepared surface so that the finished sweets are about 3 mm (⅛ in) thick.

# · SESAME SNAPS ·

*Makes about 400 g (14 oz)*

**170 g (6 oz) sesame seeds**
**225 g (8 oz) golden granulated sugar**
**4 tablespoons water**

Generously oil or butter a marble slab or metal baking sheet.

Spread the sesame seeds in a large frying pan, without added fat, and toast them lightly on a low heat. They give off a marvellously rich, nutty smell as they begin to colour.

Put the sugar and water in a small, heavy pan and heat gently until the sugar has dissolved completely. Wash down any sugar crystals from the sides of the pan with a pastry brush dipped in water. Raise the heat and boil the syrup to the hard crack stage (149°C/300°F). Take it off the heat, stir in

the seeds and immediately pour the mixture on to the prepared surface.

Before it is quite cold, mark into bars about 2 by 5 cm (¾ by
2 in). When it has set hard, break the snaps apart and store
them, individually wrapped, in an airtight container.


Pecan nuts, which are very widely available now in
wholefood shops, tend to be sweeter than walnuts and their
skins less bitter. Use perfect pecan halves to sandwich a
filling of nutty marzipan and dip the sweets in caramel to
give them a glittering, brittle coat. The same method can be
used to finish stuffed dates or prunes.

# · PECAN CANDIES ·

*Makes about 680 g (1½ lb)*

**225 g (8 oz) shelled pecan nuts**
**225 g (8 oz) marzipan (see page 16)**
**340 g (12 oz) granulated sugar**
**6 tablespoons water**

Pick out 110 g (4 oz) of perfect pecan nut halves and chop the
remainder quite finely. Mix the chopped nuts into the marzipan and roll it into balls, each about the size of a grape.
Sandwich each marzipan ball neatly between two pecan
halves.

Generously oil or butter a marble slab or metal tray. Put the
sugar in a small pan with the water and heat slowly until the
sugar has dissolved completely. Wash down any crystals
from the sides of the pan with a pastry brush dipped in cold
water. Raise the heat and boil the syrup to the hard crack stage
(149°C/300°F). Immediately dip the base of the pan in cold
water to stop the temperature rising further.

Dip the pecan and marzipan sandwiches into the hot syrup,
using a fork to lower them into the glaze. Set the dipped
candies on the prepared surface to cool. When they are quite

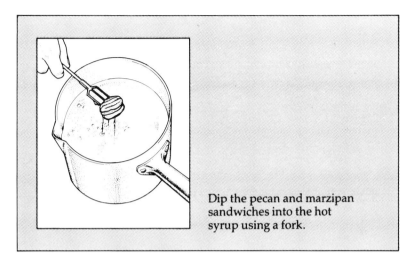

Dip the pecan and marzipan sandwiches into the hot syrup using a fork.

cold put them in individual paper cases and serve on the day they are made.

# · BUTTERED BRAZILS ·

*Makes about 225 g (8 oz)*

**110 g (4 oz) soft brown sugar**
**5 tablespoons golden syrup**
**5 tablespoons water**
**30 g (1 oz) salted butter**
**110 g (4 oz) shelled brazil nuts**

Generously oil or butter a smooth marble, metal or enamelled surface.

Put the sugar, syrup and water into a heavy pan and stir on a low heat until the sugar has dissolved completely. Wash down any crystals from the sides of the pan with a pastry brush dipped in cold water. Raise the heat and boil the syrup to the soft crack stage (140°C/305°F).

Take the pan off the heat and stir in the butter. Working quickly, dip the nuts, one at a time, using an oiled dipping or fondue fork.

Set the toffee-coated nuts on the prepared surface and leave them to cool. When they are quite cold, wrap them individually and store in an airtight container.

# · TOFFEE APPLES ·

*Makes at least 8*

**340 g (12 oz) soft brown sugar**
**225 g (8 oz) golden syrup**
**2 teaspoons vinegar**
**4 tablespoons water**
**30 g (1 oz) butter**
**8 medium-sized crisp eating apples, preferably Cox's Orange Pippins**
**8 sticks**

Put the sugar, syrup, vinegar and water into a heavy saucepan and stir over a low heat until the sugar has dissolved completely. Raise the heat and boil the mixture for about 5 minutes, or until a sugar thermometer reads 149°C/300°F, indicating that the syrup has reached the hard crack stage.

Take the pan off the heat and stir in the butter. Impale each apple on a stick and dip them, one at a time, into the molten toffee. Set the apples, sticks up, on a well-greased tin or plate and leave until quite cold.

Toffee apples are best eaten the day they are made.

Sharp fresh fruits in a coating of sweet, brittle candy are the simplest of sweets to make yet they look and taste sophisticated. Grapes and cherries are particularly suitable for dipping in clear, hard toffee. Individual segments of soft citrus fruits like tangerines and clementines can also be dipped; separate the fruit into segments and leave them to dry on a rack for up to twenty-four hours before dipping them. This drying allows the toffee to coat the pieces evenly.

Whichever fruit you dip, these sweets should always be eaten on the same day.

# · CARAMELIZED GRAPES ·

*Makes about 680 g (1½ lb)*

**450 g (1 lb) firm ripe grapes, black or green**
**450 g (1 lb) granulated sugar**
**120 ml (4 fl oz) water**

Oil or butter a tray on which to put the dipped grapes.

Separate the grapes into pairs or single fruits, leaving a short length of stem attached to each grape.

Put the sugar in a heavy pan with the water and heat slowly together until the sugar has dissolved completely. Wash down any crystals from the sides of the pan with a pastry brush dipped in cold water. Raise the heat and boil the syrup rapidly to the hard crack stage (149°C/300°F). Immediately dip the base of the pan in cold water to stop the temperature of the sugar rising higher.

Holding the grapes by their stems, preferably in tongs (sugar tongs are ideal for this job), dip them quickly into the sugar and set them on the prepared tray to harden.

If the syrup in the pan hardens before all the grapes have been dipped, it can be melted down again with a little more water then boiled up to hard crack a second time. Any syrup left over can be diluted with water and used for fruit salad or some other purpose.

Clusters of toasted hazelnuts or almonds set in a blob of brittle, nutty toffee make very good centres for dark chocolates – if you can resist eating them up before they are dipped.

## · NUT CLUSTERS ·

*Makes about 450 g (1 lb)*

**225 g (8 oz) shelled hazelnuts or almonds**
**225 g (8 oz) granulated sugar**
**5 tablespoons water**

Spread the hazelnuts on a baking tray and toast them in a preheated moderate oven (160°C/325°F, gas mark 3) for about 15 minutes, or until the centres are a pale biscuit colour. Cool the nuts and rub off their skins in a clean cloth. (If you are using almonds, remove the skins before toasting them. They will slip off easily if the nuts are soaked for one minute in boiling water.)

Finely chop half the nuts. Generously oil or butter a marble slab or metal tray.

Put the sugar and water in a small heavy pan and heat slowly together until the sugar has dissolved completely. Wash down any crystals from the sides of the pan with a pastry brush dipped in cold water. Raise the heat and boil the syrup to a light caramel (160°C/320°F). Stir in the chopped nuts.

Drop teaspoonfuls of the syrup on to the prepared surface to make individual round blobs of toffee and, while the toffee is still soft, press two or three whole nuts into each sweet. When they are cold and brittle wrap the sweets individually or dip them in dark chocolate.


A teacupful of dried maize makes a very large pan of popcorn. It is an astonishing transformation, and a quick one. The popped corn is then turned in a mixture of melted butter and syrup, and instantly it is candied. It could not be faster or easier, and of course when freshly made it tastes especially good too.

Corn for popping can be found in special packets in supermarkets, but look out for cheaper dried maize in wholefood shops.

## · CANDIED POPCORN ·

*Makes about 110 g (4 oz) – which is a lot*

**1 tablespoon vegetable oil (corn, sunflower or peanut)**
**55 g (2 oz) dried maize**
**55 g (2 oz) salted butter**
**4 tablespoons golden syrup**

Put the oil in a large pan which has a close-fitting lid. Heat until it shimmers then add the corn and immediately clamp on the lid. Cook the corn over a high heat, shaking the pan continuously and holding the lid on firmly until all the popping noises inside have stopped. Then open the pan and pour the hot, popped corn into a bowl.

In the same pan heat together the butter and syrup. When the butter has melted and the mixture is bubbling, return the popcorn to the pan and turn it quickly in the buttery mixture to coat it evenly. Pour it all out again on to a lightly greased tray and leave to cool. When it is cold the coating is crisp. Store in an airtight container.

# —6—
# Soft sweets

Fudge and truffles are more often made at home than any other types of sweet, and no wonder. They always taste terrific and are much less temperamental than many other sweet recipes. Fudge is made and sets quickly, and can be simply wrapped because it does not instantly become sticky if left in contact with the air. Truffles too demand no special treatment.

Making extra smooth cooked fondant is a trickier technique to master, but worth the effort.

Cooked fondant is a confectioner's standby, one of those useful preparations which is the basis of many finished sweets. Once made, it keeps for months, ready at a moment's notice to take on any of dozens of flavours or colours.

With cooked fondant you can make anything from the smoothest of rose cream centred chocolates to the simplest and prettiest of *petits fours*, whole fruits dipped in fondant. Grapes are available all year round and, in their seasons, cherries, strawberries and Cape gooseberries can take their turn. Cape gooseberries, which taste like tiny mangoes, are those grape-sized berries that hide inside papery shells the same shape as Chinese lantern flowers.

Cooked fondant is the greatest fun to make, but it is hard

work. Turning hot syrup into a solid yet malleable block of smoothly recrystallized sugar will take fifteen to twenty minutes of sometimes strenuous effort. One inexpensive specialized piece of equipment which can be a great help is a metal scraper with a chunky rolled metal or wooden handle. If this is not available a wooden spatula may be used instead.

# · FONDANT ·

*Makes about 400 g (14 oz)*

**450 g (1 lb) granulated sugar**
**2 tablespoons liquid glucose**
**150 ml (¼ pt) water**

To make fondant a syrup is worked with a scraper or spatula then, when cool enough to handle, it is kneaded by hand. The best surface for working it on is marble, but whichever work surface you use, sprinkle it first with water in preparation for pouring the syrup on to it.

Put the sugar, glucose and water into a medium-sized pan and heat them slowly together, stirring occasionally, until the sugar has dissolved completely. Wash down any sugar crystals from the sides of the pan with a pastry brush dipped in cold water.

Bring the syrup to the boil over a high heat and boil it to the soft ball stage (116°C/240°F). Immediately take the pan off the heat and stand it in cold water to stop the temperature rising further.

Pour the syrup on to the prepared work surface and allow it to cool for a minute or two before beginning to work it. Using a metal scraper or wooden spatula, turn the edges of the puddle of syrup into the centre to help it cool evenly. Then as it becomes thicker, work it in a figure-of-eight motion until it becomes stiff, white and crumbly.

Now the fondant must be kneaded by hand until it is smooth. Start with wet hands and continue kneading the sugar, which is hard and lumpy at first, until it becomes even-textured and plastic. Rest the fondant for at least 12 hours before moulding it. Fondant keeps best in the refrigerator, tightly wrapped in a plastic bag or tub. Stored like this it keeps almost indefinitely.

How fondant is flavoured and coloured will depend on its final use. Knead in colour and flavour if it is to be moulded by hand into simple shapes like balls or cylinders.

However, if the fondant is to be melted so that it can be poured into moulds or used for dipping, then colour and flavourings can be stirred into the melted mixture. Always melt fondant slowly over indirect heat – a bowl or pan set over

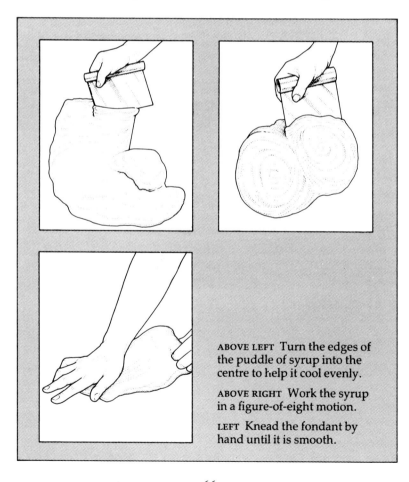

ABOVE LEFT Turn the edges of the puddle of syrup into the centre to help it cool evenly.

ABOVE RIGHT Work the syrup in a figure-of-eight motion.

LEFT Knead the fondant by hand until it is smooth.

a larger pan of simmering water – and never allow the temperature to climb above 60°C/140°F. If it is overheated it will lose its creamy texture and become hard and brittle when it sets. To make the melted fondant runny enough to pour you will need to add a tablespoon or two of extra liquid, so it can be flavoured with strong coffee, fruit purée or a liqueur, as well as with the usual range of essences.

When dipping fresh fruits into melted fondant make sure they are completely dry or the sugar coating will not stick. For this reason it is important not to puncture them, so hold them by the stalk and dip one at a time.

# · COFFEE CREAMS ·

*Makes 400 g (14 oz)*

**400 g (14 oz) ripened fondant**
**2 tablespoons instant coffee, granules or powder**
**2 tablespoons hot water**

Put the fondant in the top of a double boiler or in a bowl over a pan of boiling water. Warm it slowly, never letting the temperature of the fondant rise above 60°C/140°F, which would cause it to harden too much on cooling.

Dissolve the coffee in the hot water and stir it thoroughly into the fondant.

Pour the melted fondant into moulds using a spoon. Allow the fondant to set for several hours before turning the coffee creams out of the moulds. Dry them on a wire rack in a warm, airy place before packing them or dipping them in chocolate.

# · ROSE FONDANTS ·

*Makes 400 g (14 oz)*

**400 g (14 oz) ripened fondant**
**rose flavouring**
**red food colouring**
**icing sugar**
**candied roses to decorate**

Rose fondants can be moulded using the technique described for coffee creams (see page 67), though you will need to add about 2 tablespoons water to the fondant, or alternatively they can be cut by hand.

Turn the fondant on to a clean work surface and spread it slightly. Sprinkle a little rose flavouring and a drop or two of red food colouring on to the fondant and knead them in very thoroughly. Check the taste and add more flavouring if necessary. Gather the fondant into a ball.

Divide the fondant into four or six pieces. Sprinkle the work surface lightly with icing sugar and roll out one piece of fondant, using a sugar dusted rolling pin, to a thickness of about 1 cm (⅓ in). Use a small round or oval cutter to stamp out the sweets. Dipping the cutter in icing sugar helps to stop it sticking. Transfer the sweets to a tray lined with baking parchment to dry. Roll and cut the remaining fondant the same way, reworking the offcuts like pastry. Turn the cut sweets after an hour or two, and then again after about twelve hours in a dry, airy place. Top each fondant with a small piece of candied rose petal. Dry the sweets for at least twenty-four hours before storing them or dipping them in chocolate.

Pure maple syrup gives a true maple flavour to this lovely fudge recipe. I make it plain, but if you like nuts in fudge then the nuts to add to this recipe are pecans or walnuts. Pecans are even easier to shell than walnuts and taste much sweeter too.

## · MAPLE FUDGE ·

*Makes about 570 g (1¼ lb)*

55 g (2 oz) butter
450 g (1 lb) granulated sugar
250 ml (8 fl oz) milk
120 ml (4 fl oz) maple syrup
1 tablespoon liquid glucose
½ teaspoon salt
1 teaspoon vanilla essence

Generously butter a tin approximately 20 cm (8 in) square.

Put the sugar, milk, syrup, glucose and salt in a medium-sized saucepan and cook the mixture over a low heat until the sugar has dissolved completely. Wash the sugar crystals down the sides of the pan using a pastry brush dipped in water. Then boil the mixture without stirring until it reaches the soft ball stage (114°C/237°F). Take the pan off the heat immediately and add the rest of the butter but do not stir it in.

Cool the mixture until the bottom of the pan feels no more than warm, then add the vanilla essence and beat the syrup until it loses its gloss and begins to stiffen. Turn it at once into the prepared tin and leave to cool. When cold it can be cut into squares with a sharp knife.

Squares of fudge do not need to be individually wrapped but keep well for several weeks. Separate layers of fudge with greaseproof or waxed paper.

Tablet, or tablets, is a Scots recipe for fudge. It is a crisp rather than a chewy fudge.

# · TABLET ·

*Makes about 450 g (1 lb)*

**450 g (1 lb) granulated sugar**
**150 ml (¼ pt) single cream**
**pinch of salt**
**vanilla essence**

Butter or oil a 20-cm (8-in) square tin.

Put the sugar in a medium-sized saucepan with the cream and salt. Heat the mixture slowly, stirring until the sugar has dissolved completely. Raise the heat and boil the syrup to the firm ball stage (118°C/245°F). Stand the pan in cold water and stir in the vanilla flavouring. Beat the syrup and as it begins to grain round the edge, stir the crust into the middle.

Before the syrup is too stiff to pour smoothly, turn it into the prepared tin. If it is too highly grained it will not pour, and if not sufficiently beaten the tablet will be chewy. While it is still warm mark the tablet into squares or bars. When quite cold, cut or break it into the marked pieces and store in an airtight container.

# · RAISIN AND YOGURT FUDGE ·

*Makes about 680 g (1½ lb)*

**450 g (1 lb) golden granulated or soft brown sugar**
**300 ml (½ pt) plain yogurt**
**1 tablespoon liquid glucose**
**1 teaspoon bicarbonate of soda**
**170 g (6 oz) seedless raisins**

Butter or oil a tin about 20 cm (8 in) square.

Put the sugar in a large pan with the yogurt, glucose and bicarbonate of soda. Heat slowly until the sugar dissolves completely, washing down the sides of the pan with a pastry brush dipped in cold water to ensure that no sugar crystals remain to spoil the finished fudge.

Raise the heat and boil the fudge, stirring occasionally to prevent the mixture sticking, until it reaches the soft ball stage (113°F/235°C). Take the pan off the heat and allow the syrup to cool until the base of the pan is no more than comfortably warm. Now beat the syrup to grain the fudge and, as it begins to thicken, stir in the raisins. Pour the fudge into the prepared tin and, while it is still soft, mark it into squares. When quite cold cut it into the marked pieces and store them in an airtight container, separating the layers with greaseproof paper.

This recipe for spiced Indian fudge is named for its flavourings of cardamom and pistachio nuts, not for its provenance.

# · SPICED INDIAN FUDGE ·

*Makes about 900 g (2 lb)*

**680 g (1½ lb) golden granulated sugar**
**175 ml (6 fl oz) water**
**400-g (14-oz) tin sweetened condensed milk**
**110 g (4 oz) butter**
**110 g (4 oz) pistachio kernels, roughly chopped**
**¼ teaspoon ground cardamom seeds**

Butter or oil a tin measuring about 20 cm (8 in) square.

Put the sugar in a large saucepan with the water, condensed milk and butter and heat slowly until the sugar has dissolved completely. Wash down any sugar crystals from the sides of the pan using a pastry brush dipped in cold water. Raise the heat and boil the syrup to the soft ball stage (113°C/235°F). Take the pan off the heat and dip the base in cold water to prevent the temperature of the syrup rising higher.

Rest the syrup for a minute or two then stir in the nuts and cardamom. Beat the syrup to grain it lightly and when it begins to stiffen, pour it into the prepared tin. While it is still soft mark out the fudge in squares, and when quite cold, cut it into pieces. Store the fudge in an airtight container, separating the layers with greaseproof paper.

Walnuts and pecans are traditional additions to fudge. When these are substituted for the pistachios, vanilla essence takes the place of the cardamom flavouring.

# · COCONUT ICE ·

*Makes about 680 g (1½ lb)*

**450 g (1 lb) granulated sugar**
**150 ml (¼ pt) fresh milk**
**170 g (6 oz) desiccated coconut**

Butter or oil a tin measuring about 20 cm (8 in) square.

Put the sugar in a heavy pan with the milk and heat slowly until the sugar has dissolved. Wash down any sugar crystals from the sides of the pan with a pastry brush dipped in cold water. Raise the heat and boil the syrup to the soft ball stage

OPPOSITE *Sweets, from centre: milk chocolate covered truffles, chocolate peppermint creams, rose creams, toffee and fudge centred chocolates, whisky truffles in dark chocolate, and chocolate peppermint creams.*

OVERLEAF *Sweets, from left: basket of rose marshmallows and apple pastilles, dish of quince pastilles, brass dish of Turkish delight, and a dish of blackcurrant jellies and quick lime jellies.*

(116°C/240°F). Immediately remove the pan from the heat and stir in the coconut.

Pour the mixture at once into the prepared tin and when it has cooled a little, mark the coconut ice into squares. Wait until it is completely cold before cutting.

If you want to make traditional pink and white coconut ice have ready a few drops of red food colouring. Pour half the white coconut ice mixture into the prepared tin, then colour the rest and pour it over the first layer.

## • CHOCOLATE TRUFFLES •

*Makes about 225 g (8 oz)*

**110 g (4 oz) dark chocolate**
**85 g (3 oz) butter**
**1 tablespoon icing sugar**
**1 tablespoon orange liqueur, rum, brandy or strong coffee**
**1 egg yolk**
**55 g (2 oz) cocoa powder or chocolate vermicelli**

In a double boiler, or a bowl set over a pan of hot water, melt together the chocolate, butter, icing sugar and liqueur or coffee. Stir well until the chocolate has melted completely then remove the pan from the heat. Allow the mixture to cool before stirring in the egg yolk. Set the mixture aside until it is completely cold.

Form the chocolate paste into balls and roll them in cocoa powder or chocolate vermicelli until they are coated on all sides. Store in a cool place. Set the truffles in fluted paper cases to serve or box.

OPPOSITE *Sweets, from left: tablet, spiced Indian fudge, chocolate fudge, maple fudge, apricot, lemon, rose, vanilla and violet creams.*

OVERLEAF *Sweets, from left: toot, raspberry and lime real fruit drops, honey nougat, coconut ice and lolliberrypops.*

These whisky truffles are a little firmer than the last recipe.

## · WHISKY TRUFFLES ·

*Makes about 225 g (8 oz)*

**170 g (6 oz) dark chocolate**
**3 tablespoons double cream**
**2 tablespoons whisky**
**1 egg yolk**
**55 g (2 oz) drinking chocolate**

Equal quantities of icing sugar and cocoa mixed make an alternative to drinking chocolate powder for the coating.

In a double boiler, or a bowl set over a pan of hot water, melt together the chocolate, cream and whisky. Stir well until the mixture is completely smooth, then cool it a little before beating in the egg yolk.

Chill the mixture before forming the paste into balls and rolling them in the drinking chocolate powder.

# —7—
# Melting sweets

It is only fitting that the finest Turkish delight should be made in Istanbul in Turkey, or so it is claimed. In fact Turkish delight is popular throughout the Middle East and family recipes for special versions of *rahat lokum* are well guarded.

Like the other melting sweets – marshmallows, fruit jujubes and pastilles – home-made Turkish delight is a revelation. As always, it is fresh ingredients as well as the cook's skills which make it taste so much more interesting than many commercial varieties. The classic flavourings of rosewater and pistachio nuts evoke pictures of harems and languorous beauties whiling away idle hours with platefuls of Turkish delight.

Its uniquely unctuous texture is produced by cooking together a mixture of sugar, starch and gum or gelatine, then flavouring it delicately with rosewater, citrus fruit or, oddly, crème de menthe. Rose-scented Turkish delight packed with pistachios or walnuts is irresistible.

# · TURKISH DELIGHT ·

*Makes about 1 kg (2¼ lb)*

**juice and grated rind of 2 lemons**
**900 g (2 lb) granulated sugar**
**110 g (4 oz) cornflour**
**45 g (1½ oz) gelatine**

Put the lemon rind, juice and sugar in a pan with 200 ml (⅓ pt) water and heat until the sugar has dissolved completely. Wash down the sugar crystals from the sides of the pan with a pastry brush dipped in cold water. Boil the syrup to the thread stage (110°C/230°F).

While the syrup is cooking soften the gelatine in about 8 tablespoons of cold water.

Whisk the dry cornflour into the syrup then gradually add the softened gelatine. Bring the mixture back to the boil and boil for 10 minutes, stirring to prevent it from catching.

Strain the liquid and pour it into two 20-cm (8-in) square

tins, or into one larger tin which has been prepared with a sprinkling of cold water. Leave the Turkish delight to set for at least 24 hours.

Liberally sprinkle a worksurface with sifted icing sugar which has been mixed with a little cornflour. Turn out the Turkish delight on to the prepared surface. Cut it into large cubes and roll them in the sugar mixture. Store the sweets in an airtight container with sheets of waxed or greaseproof paper between each layer.

Marsh mallow, a downy grey-green plant with pink flowers, was for centuries eaten as a vegetable, and the mucilage (gummy or gelatinous secretion) from its roots, long an ingredient of soothing cough syrups, was responsible for the name of the sweet. Nowadays the sweets are made without any help from the marshmallow plant. Some modern recipes call for gum arabic to be included, but most rely on a mixture of gelatine and egg white to give the marshmallows their distinctive springy texture.

# · MARSHMALLOWS ·

*Makes about 570 g (1¼ lb)*

**450 g (1 lb) granulated sugar**
**1 tablespoon liquid glucose**
**350 ml (12 fl oz) water**
**30 g (1 oz) gelatine crystals**
**2 egg whites**
**orange flower water or rosewater**
**icing sugar and cornflour to dust**

Prepare a tin about 30 by 20 cm (12 by 8 in) by lining it with non-stick baking parchment dusted lightly with cornflour.

Put the sugar in a medium-sized pan with the glucose and 250 ml (8 fl oz) of the water. Heat gently until the sugar has dissolved completely. Wash any sugar crystals from the sides of the pan with a pastry brush dipped in water. Raise the heat and boil the syrup to the hard ball stage (124°C/255°F).

While the syrup is cooking, prepare the gelatine by soaking it in a small pan with the remaining water, and when it is soft and swollen, heat the mixture gently to dissolve the crystals.

Whisk the egg whites to a stiff meringue in a large, preferably copper bowl.

When the syrup is ready, take it off the heat and stir in the gelatine mixture and one or two tablespoons of orange flower water or rosewater.

Now pour the syrup into the meringue in a thin steady stream, whisking continuously until the mixture forms a thick white cloud of dense marshmallow. Before it becomes too stiff to pour smoothly, turn the marshmallow into the prepared tin and smooth the top flat with a palette knife. Leave the sweet to set, preferably overnight.

Turn the marshmallow out of its tin on to a work surface dusted with icing sugar mixed with a little cornflour. Cut into cubes and dust them on all sides with the sugar and cornflour mixture. Leave to dry for an hour or so before packing them in an airtight container.

Toasted marshmallows are the traditional ending to any barbecue or bonfire picnic. Everyone should toast their own by spiking a marshmallow on the end of a stick or fondue fork and holding it close to the heat, turning it steadily as it swells and bubbles. Toasted marshmallows are ready when the outside has browned to a pale crust and the inside is just melting.

Jujubes sound more amusing than jellies which is what these sweets are more usually called now. Make them with the fresh juice of strongly flavoured fruits like blackcurrants, raspberries, limes, oranges or lemons.

To make the most of the flavour in blackcurrants or raspberries, put the berries in a large pan without additional liquid. Cover and heat the fruit gently until the juices run; this will take ten to fifteen minutes. Stir the fruit from time to time, then strain it through a fine sieve. The debris can be used to flavour muesli, or for some other purpose. Each 450 g (1 lb) of fruit will yield about 150 ml (¼ pt) of juice.

# · BLACKCURRANT JUJUBES ·

*Makes about 450 g (1 lb)*

**300 ml (½ pt) fresh blackcurrant juice (see above)**
**225 g (8 oz) granulated sugar**
**6 tablespoons liquid glucose (optional – see method)**
**55 g (2 oz) gelatine crystals**
**4 tablespoons water**
**4 tablespoons fresh lemon juice**
**caster sugar to coat**

Put the blackcurrant juice, sugar and glucose into a pan and heat them slowly together until the sugar has dissolved completely. The glucose gives the jellies a chewier texture than they would have without it.

Sprinkle the gelatine on to the water and lemon juice mixed, and when it has swollen and softened, stir it into the fruit syrup. Heat the mixture gently until the gelatine too has dissolved completely.

Wet a 20-cm (8-in) square tin with cold water and pour the syrup into it. Leave the jelly to set in a cool place for several hours, or overnight.

Turn the slab of jelly on to a cutting surface and use a sharp knife to cut it into diamond-shaped lozenges or cubes, or petits fours cutters to stamp out more exotic shapes. Roll the sweets in sugar to finish them.

Store the jujubes in an airtight container with sheets of greaseproof paper separating the layers of sweets.

Citrus fruits are simply halved and squeezed to extract their juice, but remember to strain it for brilliantly clear jellies. For greater intensity of flavour, use the very old technique of rubbing the fruit rind with sugar cubes to extract the oil from the zest. The sugar will soak up the oil and can then be used to sweeten the jellies.

Many cooks hesitate to use fresh zest because they know that most citrus fruit is treated with a fungicidal wax before it reaches this country. The treatment is said by the Ministry of Agriculture to be safe and there seems to be no body of opinion to the contrary. Incidentally, Seville oranges, the bitter oranges for marmalade-making that are on sale in January and February, are untreated.

High quality commercial cordials can also be used to make jellies. Blackcurrant and lime cordials are the most easily obtained.

# · QUICK LIME JELLIES ·

*Makes about 450 g (1 lb)*

**300 ml (½ pt) undiluted lime cordial**
**225 g (8 oz) granulated sugar**
**55 g (2 oz) gelatine crystals**
**sugar to dredge**

Put the cordial in a small pan with the sugar and heat slowly until the sugar has dissolved completely. Wash down any sugar crystals sticking to the sides of the pan with a pastry brush dipped in cold water.

Sprinkle the gelatine on to 120 ml (4 fl oz) cold water and leave it until it has swollen and softened. Add the softened gelatine to the lime syrup and stir the mixture on a low heat until the gelatine has dissolved completely.

Wet a 20-cm (8-in) square tin with cold water and pour in the syrup. Leave it in a cool place to set for several hours or overnight.

Turn the slab of jelly on to a cutting surface and use a sharp knife or petits fours cutters to fashion it into plain or fancy shapes. Roll the cut sweets in granulated sugar to coat them on all sides.

An alternative method of shaping the sweets is to pour the syrup into a hard rubber fondant mould, or into the newer clear plastic moulds sold for shaping chocolates. To unmould the jellies use a thumb or finger to loosen one corner by stroking the base of the sweet. Then when the corner can be lifted, the sweet can be pulled out slowly without breaking.

Marmalade started life as a confection of dried quince paste and not as the orange jam we call marmalade now. These fruit pastes are among the oldest types of sweet known and they consist simply of puréed fruit cooked with sugar until it is firm enough to set well when cooled. Soft fruits like strawberries and raspberries need no preliminary cooking and can be puréed raw, but apples need cooking before they can be pulped. This helps to extract the pectin which will make the confection set. The addition of fresh lemon juice will help to set the sweets too.

Quinces have so much pectin that they are the easiest of fruits to turn into home made pastilles. Ripe quinces are pale yellow rather than green and have a pleasant perfume. They are still as hard as the unripe fruit.

# · QUINCE PASTILLES ·

*Makes about 680 g (1½ lb)*

680 g (1½ lb) ripe quinces
150 ml (¼ pt) white wine or water
450 g (1 lb) granulated sugar
juice of 2 lemons
1 teaspoon ground cinnamon
½ teaspoon ground cloves
granulated sugar to dredge (see method)

Chop the quinces coarsely without peeling or coring them and put the pieces in a pan with the wine or water. Cook them gently, covered, until the pulp is soft enough to pass easily through a sieve. Strain the purée. Wash the pan and butter or oil a 20-cm (8-in) square tin. Use a non-stick tin if you have it.

Return the purée to the pan and add the sugar, lemon juice and spice. Simmer the purée steadily, stirring it often, until it is very thick. Pay great attention to the paste as it thickens because it tends to stick to the base of the pan and may easily burn. It is ready when a spoon drawn through the mixture leaves a permanent groove.

Spread the paste in the prepared tin and leave it to set for at least 24 hours. Then, except if you plan to use the paste as a filling for chocolates, turn it on to a surface which has been generously dusted with granulated sugar. Leave the quince paste to dry in a warm, airy place for at least 24 hours more before cutting it into individual sweets.

Flat squares are a traditional shape for pastilles, but using a set of canapé cutters, circles, hearts, leaves and many more shapes are possible. Dredge the pastilles in sugar and leave them until they are quite dry before packing them.

Quince paste intended for use as chocolate centres should be dried thoroughly without extra sugar before being dipped.

# · APPLE PASTILLES ·

*Makes about 680 g (1½ lb)*

680 g (1½ lb) cooking apples
150 ml (¼ pt) apple juice, white wine or water
450 g (1 lb) granulated sugar
juice of 2 lemons
½ teaspoon mixed spice
caster sugar to dredge

Chop the apples coarsely without peeling or coring them and put in a pan with the apple juice, wine or water. Cook gently, covered, until the apples are soft then press through a sieve or purée them in a *mouli légumes*.

Wash the pan and butter or oil a 20-cm (8-in) square tin.

Return the purée to the pan and add the sugar, lemon juice and spice. Simmer the purée steadily, stirring it often, until it is very thick. Pay great attention towards the end of cooking when the stiffening paste catches and burns on the bottom of the pan.

Spread the paste in the prepared tin and leave it to set for at least twenty-four hours. Turn it out, and if necessary dry it for a further twenty-four hours in a warm, airy place before cutting it into individual sweets. Flat squares are a traditional shape for fruit pastes, but the pastilles can be stamped out with round or fancy cutters. Dredge the sweets with sugar before storing them in an airtight container.

# —8—
# Chocolate assortment

Making chocolates is uniquely rewarding because the results look so immensely professional while the tastes have all the extra richness of centres made with fresh ingredients.

The rules for successful chocolate making are few but vital. Most important of all is the quality of the chocolate used whether it be plain, milk or white.

Professional confectioners use a top quality chocolate called *couverture* which contains a very high proportion of cocoa butter. Because the fats contained in cocoa butter are particularly unstable, *couverture* has to be tempered by heating and cooling it to carefully controlled temperatures. In practised hands it gives the finest results in terms of both taste and appearance, and enthusiastic chocolate makers will certainly want to try it eventually. *Couverture* is available from confectionery suppliers (see pages 10–11), and tempering instructions are included with the chocolate.

Most cooks are more than happy with the results that are possible using the unprepossessing-looking dipping chocolate, sold by an increasing number of specialist kitchen shops, or with good dessert chocolate available everywhere. What will not do for confectionery are the cheaper blocks of soft baking chocolate and chocolate flavoured coating bars to be found in every supermarket. Neither their taste nor their texture is good enough for sweets.

The secret of successful chocolate handling is temperature control. Essentially this means melting chocolate slowly over indirect heat and never allowing the thermometer to rise above 49°C (120°F). Overheating it can result in a grey bloom on the finished sweets.

Keeping moisture out of the melted chocolate is also critical. Even a few puffs of steam can cause it to seize or stiffen irreparably, so always melt it in a wide bowl set over a smaller pan of hot water.

If all this makes chocolate dipping and moulding sound intimidating, don't be put off. Any chocolate which has been accidentally damaged by heat or damp can be used for flavouring truffles or other sweets. And this leads me to the most useful piece of advice on the subject of dipping, which is to melt a considerably larger quantity of chocolate than you will need for the job in hand. It is much easier to work with a large pool of molten chocolate than with a skimpy puddle, and a large amount is less likely to be overheated accidentally. Nothing is wasted because the unused chocolate can be left to harden then stored in an airtight container and used again.

Smoothly dipped chocolates may be based on centres of every type. A three- and four-pronged chocolate dipping fork is a help because its thin tines and straight shape are designed to allow the covered centres to slip off easily. However, a table fork can, of course, be used instead.

The easiest chocolates to practise dipping are those with relatively hard centres like caramels. Then, when you have mastered the art of lifting the centres cleanly out of the molten chocolate, the time has come to dip fondants, and finally, fragile sandwiched fillings.

The traditional patterns on chocolates of bars and loops are made by marking the setting chocolates with the dipping fork or another confectioner's tool, the dipping ring. Rose and violet creams are invariably topped with chips of crystallized rose or violet petals, but there is no need to continue the custom. Silver dragees, small pieces of crystallized fruit, nuts and sugared flowers of every sort can be used to make your personal chocolate assortment.

# · CHOCOLATE CARAMELS ·

*Makes about 450 g (1 lb)*

**dark chocolate for dipping**
**340 g (12 oz) vanilla caramels (see page 43)**

Break the chocolate into a wide bowl and set it over a pan of hot water to melt. Stir the chocolate as it melts and do not let the temperature rise above 49°C/120°F. Allow the chocolate to cool and begin to thicken a little before dipping the caramels.

Dip the caramels one at a time into the chocolate and set

them on a tray lined with greaseproof paper to harden. As the chocolate begins to stiffen use the dipping fork to mark a pattern of bars on the top of the sweets.

When the chocolate has set hard, put the sweets in paper cases and store them in a cool place.

Both cooked and uncooked fondant make excellent peppermint creams to coat lavishly with dark chocolate. Cooked fondant centres (see pages 64–7) are smoother, but peppermint creams made with uncooked fondant (see page 21) are equally good. In either case the fondant shapes should be stamped out and dried for twenty-four hours before coating.

## · CHOCOLATE PEPPERMINT · CREAMS

*Makes about 450 g (1 lb)*

**dark chocolate for dipping**
**340 g (12 oz) peppermint creams (see page 21 and above)**

Break the chocolate into a wide bowl and set it over a pan of hot water to melt. Stir the chocolate as it melts and do not let the temperature rise above 49°C/120°F. Allow the chocolate to cool a little and thicken slightly before dipping the centres.

Dip the peppermint creams, one at a time, into the molten chocolate and set them on a tray lined with greaseproof paper. As the chocolate begins to harden and becomes tacky enough to hold the pattern, draw a dipping fork across each chocolate to mark it with a pattern of bars. Alternatively, a ring-shaped dipping tool can be used to mark circles on the sweets.

When the chocolates have hardened well, set them in paper cases and store in a cool place.

*Petits fours*-sized florentines (crisp nutty wafers with chocolate on one side) come somewhere between sweets and biscuits. I prefer florentines to after dinner mints, especially when the chocolates are served with coffee. Hazelnuts can be substituted for the almonds.

# · FLORENTINES ·

*Makes about 50*

55 g (2 oz) butter
6 tablespoons double cream
110 g (4 oz) golden granulated sugar
110 g (4 oz) flaked almonds
110 g (4 oz) chopped almonds
110 g (4 oz) glacé cherries, quartered
55 g (2 oz) candied orange peel, finely chopped
finely grated zest of 1 orange
55 g (2 oz) flour
¼ teaspoon salt
225 g (8 oz) dark chocolate

Put the butter, cream and sugar in a heavy pan and heat, stirring, until the sugar dissolves. Bring the mixture to the boil then remove the pan from the heat. Stir in the almonds, cherries, peel, zest, flour and salt. Mix well.

Drop small spoonfuls of the mixture on to buttered or non-stick baking sheets, spacing the florentines well apart. Use a wet knife to flatten each biscuit before baking in a preheated moderate oven (180°C/350°F, gas mark 4) for twelve to fifteen minutes, or until they are starting to brown at the edges. While they are still warm transfer the florentines to a wire rack to cool.

Break the chocolate into small pieces and put in a wide bowl over a small pan of hot water. Allow the chocolate to melt without additional liquid and use it to spread on one side of each florentine. As it begins to set use a clean comb to make the traditional pattern of wavy lines in the chocolate.

Florentines will keep fresh for several weeks if they are stored in an airtight container.

The complaint about chocolate today is that the quality is not as good as it used to be. This is undoubtedly true of many mass market chocolate bars if not of the best and, inevitably, most expensive chocolate. But at least we can buy ready made chocolate. William Gunter, writing *Gunter's Confectioner's Oracle* in 1830, started with the cocoa beans.

'Roast the kernels, stirring them well, and deprive them of all *husk*. Reduce them to a *paste* in a *hot* iron mortar. Use the proportions of 12 lbs cocoa to 8 lbs sugar; and after adding the sugar, still keep working the mixture in the mortar: put the whole in a *hot* place, and on a *hot flat stone*, with a metal roller, laminate half-a-pound (adding an ounce or two of *pulverized* vanilla, if it is to be so flavoured); and when all is done well, and with expedition, and is perfectly reduced to a dissoluble paste, put it into small moulds, from which eject when it is cold.'

I have the distinct impression that we are the winners here, and that our chocolate tastes a great deal better than Mr Gunter's did. He lamented contemporary English standards in the following footnote: 'They take infinitely more pains in the manufacture of chocolate in Paris than London, and consequently have it of a very superior description. There is an impatience about the English in operations chiefly manual, that injures most of their processes. It is also to be remarked, however, that *more* chocolate is drunk in France than in this country: the people there *bathe* about three times a week, and always take a cup of Vanilla chocolate before quitting the warm water.'

William Gunter's recipe for chocolate drops is interesting for the variety of flavours he suggests.

'Drops in chocolate are made by simply forcing chocolate paste into small moulds, after having flavoured it with any desired essence, or a combination of aromatic materials such as vanilla, cloves, ambergris, and cinnamon, with a small additional portion of sugar, double refined and pulverized.'

The pattern of sharp peaks on the coating of milk chocolate truffles is achieved by rolling the chocolates across a wire rack as they cool.

# · RICH MILK ·
# CHOCOLATE TRUFFLES

*Makes about 340 g (12 oz)*

**170 g (6 oz) milk chocolate**
**30 g (1 oz) butter**
**2 egg yolks**
**milk chocolate for dipping**

Break the 170 g (6 oz) milk chocolate into small pieces and put in a bowl over a pan of hot water. When the chocolate has melted take the bowl off the heat and beat in the butter and egg yolks. Chill the mixture until it is firm enough to handle.

Form teaspoonfuls of the chocolate mixture into small, evenly-sized balls, and lay them on a tray lined with grease-proof paper. Chill well.

Melt the dipping chocolate in a wide bowl over a smaller pan of hot water, being careful that the temperature of the chocolate goes no higher than 49°C/120°F. Allow the chocolate to cool and thicken a little then use it to coat the prepared truffle centres. Dip them into the chocolate one at a time and

91

transfer to a wire rack. As the chocolate coating begins to stiffen, use a fork to roll each truffle once or twice across the rack to give its surface a characteristically peaky finish.

Store the finished truffles in a cool place.

Plain dark chocolate may be substituted for milk chocolate either for the truffle filling or for the coating, or for both. The truffles can also be used as centres for dipping.

Nut and raisin clusters are very easy chocolates to make. They call for juicy raisins (preferably stoned muscatels) and fresh nuts. Very coarsely chopped almonds or lightly toasted hazels are particularly good, and pecans and currants are another tasty combination.

# · NUT AND RAISIN CLUSTERS ·

*Makes about 450 g (1 lb)*

**110 g (4 oz) seedless raisins**
**110 g (4 oz) toasted hazelnuts (see page 60)**
**225 g (8 oz) dark chocolate**
**dark chocolate for dipping**

Put the raisins and coarsely chopped nuts into a bowl and mix them well.

Break the 225 g (8 oz) dark chocolate into a bowl and set it over a pan of hot water to melt. Stir the melted chocolate into the nut and raisin mixture until well combined. Use two teaspoons to form blobs of the fruit and nut mixture on a tray lined with greaseproof paper. Leave the clusters to set hard.

Melt the dipping chocolate in a wide bowl over a smaller pan of hot water, being careful that the temperature of the chocolate does not rise above 49°C/120°F. Allow the chocolate to cool and thicken a little before dipping the nut clusters and setting them to dry on a sheet of greaseproof paper. When the clusters are quite hard set them in paper cases and store in a cool place.

# · CHOCOLATE CUPS ·

Fluted metal chocolate cases are stronger than the more usual paper ones, and because they are tougher it is much easier to use them for making chocolate cups. These can be fashioned from plain, milk or white chocolate and any kind of filling you fancy. Hot fondant can be poured into cups already lined with molten chocolate and allowed to set, or the cups can be primed with a nut or two and chocolate poured in afterwards.

Another kind of chocolate cup which is especially good is a dark chocolate shell filled with a blob of chocolate truffle mixture piped through a star-nozzle. In this case fluted metal or paper cases are partly filled with melted chocolate and turned upside down to drain and harden. Then the cases are peeled away and the resulting shells are ready to fill.

An American idea which might well catch on elsewhere is that of filling the shells with single cream and serving them with after dinner black coffee – the cream and its chocolate container are stirred into the hot coffee.

# · EASTER EGGS ·

Easter eggs are the biggest chocolates you are ever likely to make. Clear, bendy plastic moulds are easier to use than traditional metal ones. They are also cheaper and produce wonderfully glossy, professional results. They are quite commonly available now in kitchen shops as well as from specialized confectionery suppliers.

For Easter eggs it is essential to use hard, top quality chocolate because the moulded shapes must be able to withstand a certain amount of handling. An excellent tip is to use wide strips of cellophane or greaseproof paper to hold the pieces whenever you need to pick them up. Good and properly tempered chocolate is slower to melt in your fingers than softer types, but it does take fingermarks quite easily.

Start by polishing the inside of both halves of the mould

with a soft dry cloth, and lay out a sheet of greaseproof paper. Melt the chocolate. Pour some melted chocolate into one mould and carefully swirl it out to the edges to coat the inside completely. Pour the excess chocolate back into the pan, and when no more chocolate will drip back, invert the coated mould on to the greaseproof paper for the chocolate to harden. Fill the other half the same way.

As one thin layer of chocolate will not be strong enough, this process should be repeated once or twice more, ensuring each time that the chocolate in the moulds has hardened completely before the next layer is added.

Don't be tempted to hurry by having one thick layer because this does not give good results. The chocolate shrinks as it cools (another reason for using clear plastic moulds is that you can see when this has occurred) and when it is quite cold the mould can be peeled off.

To join the two half shells spread the edges with melted chocolate and press them together. Cover the join with a pretty ribbon or, if you are feeling more ambitious, use a fancy icing nozzle to pipe a continuous pattern round the egg to cover the join.

Chocolate Easter eggs are traditionally filled with chocolates, but why not surprise someone small by hiding a toy inside, or someone you love with a letter, a tiny volume of poetry, or a jewel.

# Index